Flying Forts
and
Tall Dutch Tulips:
A Year at War

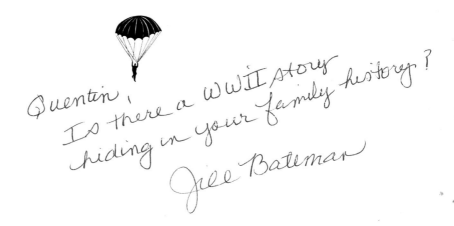

Quentin,
Is there a WWII story
hiding in your family history?
Jill Bateman

Jill Bateman

Maple Avenue Press
LLC

Maple Avenue Press
LLC
3207 Harrisburg Pike
Landisville, Pennsylvania 17538
U.S.A.

Printed in the United States by
Intelligencer Printing, Lancaster, Pennsylvania.

First Edition, 2015.

Cataloging Data
Bateman, Jill.
Flying Forts and Tall Dutch Tulips: A Year at War / Jill Bateman. — 1st ed.
p.   cm.
ISBN 978-1-4951-8052-1
ISBN 978-1-4951-8053-8 (pbk.)

1. Bateman, Jill — Juvenile literature.
2. Holocaust, Jewish (1939-1945) — Netherlands — Juvenile literature.
3. World War, 1939-1945 — Prisoners and prisons, German — Juvenile
literature.
4. World War, 1939-1945 — Netherlands — Juvenile literature.
5. World War, 1939-1945 — United States — Juvenile literature.
6. Netherlands — History — German occupation — Juvenile literature.
7. United States — History — World War, 1939-1945 — Juvenile literature.
8. United States. Army Air Force. Bombardment Group (H), 401st — History
— Juvenile literature.
9. Westerbork (Netherlands: Concentration camp) — Juvenile literature.
10. Airplanes, Military — World War, 1939-1945 — Juvenile literature.

I. Title.
940.5

Flying Forts and Tall Dutch Tulips
is an international story.

Dates in Europe are written
first with the day, then the month, and year:
29 April 1944.

Time in much of Europe and in the
United States military services
runs on a twenty-four hour clock:
24:00 hours is midnight.
01:00 hours is 1:00 am.
13:00 hours is 1:00 pm.
18:30 hours is 6:30 pm and so on.
(USA military time does not use the colon.)

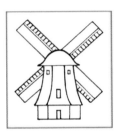

The Netherlands is the official name of the country
where much of this story took place. Its nickname is
Holland, which comes from the names of two of its
twelve provinces: North Holland and South Holland.
People living here are called Dutch, and so is their
language. The country is known for its tulips,
windmills, and cheese.

Pronunciation of Dutch Names

Ab: ab
Arnhem: 'ärn-hem
Bep: bep
Bosman: 'bōs-man
Deelen: 'dē-len
Dien: dēn
Dieren: 'dēr-en
Diet: dēt
De Steeg: de 'stēg
Ellecom: 'ell-e-com
The Hague: the 'hāg
Jan: yon
Joop: yōp
Levie: 'lev-ē
Nel: nel

In the early 1920s, a madman became determined to avenge Germany's defeat in World War I. Adolf Hitler's Nazi Party, led by thugs, bullies, and murderers, began winning and rigging elections until Hitler became Chancellor of Germany in 1933.

That was not enough for Hitler. With dreams of creating an empire that would rule for a thousand years, he sent war planes, paratroops, tanks, and thousands of goose-stepping soldiers sweeping across Europe.

By 1941, Allied forces from six continents were embroiled in a second world war — combating Hitler's aggression in Europe and that of Japan in the Pacific.

One of the European countries that fell to Nazi forces was the Netherlands. The Dutch people found themselves under the command of the *Schutzstaffel,* brutal *SS* troops that also had orders from Hitler to rid Europe of its Jews whom he blamed for Germany's loss in 1918.

Flemington, New Jersey
U.S.A.
Fall, 1950

A little girl,
with hair straight as a ruler,
stood on a wooden chair.
She was helping Mommy and Daddy
stuff a big carton for a Dutch family
who lived w-a-a-a-y
across the ocean from America.

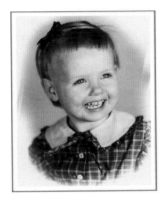

The nice Dutch family
had played hide-and-seek
with Daddy in the war.

She asked Daddy what a war was.

He said she needed
to grow some
before he told her about war.

She and Mommy packed the box
with cans of powdered milk.
Sugar.
Tea.
Coffee.
Cigarettes
and tobacco like Gramps smoked in his pipe.
Huge bars of Hershey chocolate.
Sweaters. Skirts. A pair of trousers.

Then she and Daddy
tucked in cakes of Ivory soap.
More chocolate would have been yummier.

A letter sat on top.
Mommy slipped a picture of her inside,
so the faraway people could see
how big she was getting.

Round and round
went scratchy twine —
to keep the cardboard box from
falling apart on its long trip.

That night,
the little girl nestled
in bed with her Raggedy Ann doll.
She yawned
and wondered
how much she had to grow
before Daddy would tell her about war.

Ellecom, Netherlands
29 April 1944
04:00 hours

Blackness.
No glowing candles.
No shining street lamps.
No twinkling starlight from on high.
Just blackness.
As if four years of war had sucked the light —
and life — out of the tiny Dutch village.

Ellecom's houses, big and small,
huddled in the darkness.
All stood silent.
Still.

All, that is, except one.

In one house,
a large brick house
with attic gables high above the street,
a candle flickered.
A wooden stair creaked.

A slight figure crept down
    steep
       cellar
          steps.

Though it was nearly May,
Dien Bosman
clutched her wool sweater closer
to keep out the cold, musty air.

Setting her candlestick down with care
on the bottom step,
Dien paused
to listen
for footsteps overhead.

Nothing.

She slipped
into the gloomy shadows
and began lifting black lumps —
one at a time —
off a mountain of coal
dumped on the dusty floor
behind the stairs.

The enemy owned the coal.

Before German tanks and paratroops
brought war
to the Netherlands in 1940,
the house known as *Benvenuto*
had welcomed vacationers from across Europe
to its comfortable rooms
and gardens
of tall, bright tulips.

The Dutch word for inn is *pension*. *Benvenuto* means welcome in Italian.

Now a German army medical staff
occupied most of its second-floor
sleeping rooms.
Twice a day,
sick German soldiers
and Dutch collaborators working
with the enemy
tramped into a first-floor examining room
for medical care.

Careful
not to get
tell-tale smudges on her clothing,
Dien stole as much coal
as she dared.

Spring nights were still bitter.

Up on the top floor,
the heating stove in the room where
her teenage daughters Bep and Diet slept
and the stoves in the two hidden rooms
where the Levies slept
gobbled up coal like it was licorice.
Her cookstove was greedy,
as well.

The iron scuttle full,
Dien tiptoed up the steps.

Careful… don't trip.
If the heavy scuttle
and candlestick
clatter
down the steps,
the Germans will leap out of bed
and catch themselves a thief.

Nazis shoot thieves.

At the top, she stopped to listen.

Not a sound.

The Germans
still slumbered overhead.

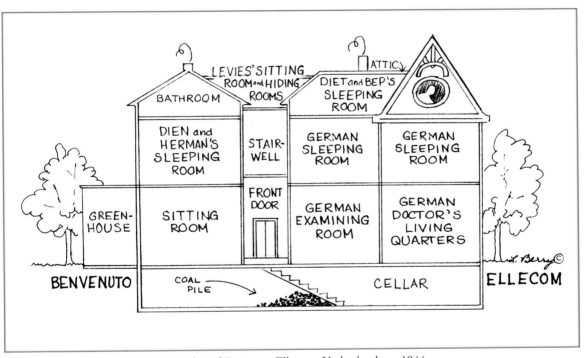

Floor plan of *Benvenuto*, Ellecom, Netherlands — 1944.

Eighth Air Force Base 128
Deenethorpe, England
29 April 1944
0640 hours

TH-WUMP!
A blood-red flare
arced through the hazy sky.
High over B-17 Flying Fortresses
parked on circular, black hardstands
clustering around Deenethorpe's
three runways.

The day's mission
was now underway
for eighteen bombers
assigned to the 401st Bombardment Group.
Three spare planes stood ready, as well.

"Start number one."

On the pilot's command,
the far left engine of the B-17 —
dubbed The Saint and Ten Sinners —
came to life
with an ear-piercing whine.

Heavy metal gears clanked.
Sparks and dark smoke
streamed back over the left wing.

The Saint and Ten Sinners - serial # 42-31226. 3 black
crosses on left show its crews had shot down 3 German
fighters. White bombs indicate 17 bombing missions had
been completed when photograph was taken.

The plane's thin aluminum skin
vibrated as the propeller
whirled faster.
FASTER.

On the plane's flight deck,
"Butter" —
officially 2nd Lt. Donald Earl Butterfoss
of the U.S. Army Air Corps,
a twenty-two-year-old
from New Jersey
who'd rather be smacking a baseball
than fighting a war —
gave his copilot
the order
to start
the second engine.

As pilot, Butter was
commander of his crew
in the air and on the ground.

In the rear fuselage,
amid the stink of hot smoky oil,
crewmen felt the plane's vibrations
drill
deep
into their bones.

Bracing themselves,
they were ready to grab fire extinguishers
should the Saint go nose-down
on take-off.

Oxygen masks dangling from necks
like religious medallions.
Parachute packs and harnesses.
Bright yellow life-jackets.
Fleece-lined gloves,
boots,
and leather hats
with built-in headphones.

Blue "bunny" suits —
electrically-heated flight suits —
worn over long-woolen underwear,
no matter
the time of year.

All were necessary battle gear
for fighting a war
in an unpressurized plane
five miles up in what
airmen
called the High Cold.
Way up yonder,
where dark blue was the color of the sky
and temperatures plummeted
to fifty degrees
below
zero.

As engine three,
then engine four spun to life,
Butter slammed a door
on his fears.
He had a job to do —
drop bombs on the day's target,
then get his crew home.

The bomber trembled and roared,
straining at its brakes like
a howling tornado
bucking against

an invisible
leash.

Easing up on the brakes,
Butter taxied into his assigned position
in the line of Flying Fortresses
bouncing
and shimmying toward runway 33.

B-17s of the 381st Bomb Group in line for take-off from
Ridgewell, England.

A newspaper reporter had given the B-17
its name, Flying Fortress,
when the first one
rolled out of the factory in 1935.
The B-17 had been living up to the name
ever since.

Bullets
from its twelve machine guns
could strafe enemy fighters

from all directions.

Its rugged framework
and powerful engines
allowed it
to bring crews home,
despite gaping holes in wings
and tails —
even a missing engine or two.

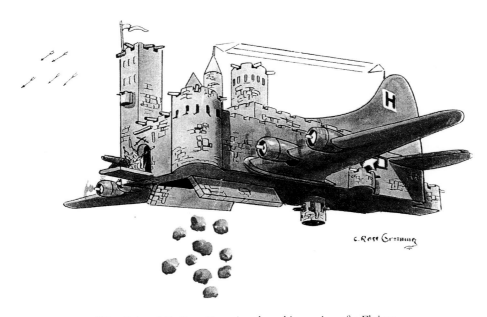

Pilot Colonel C. Ross Greening drew his version of a Flying
Fortress while imprisoned at Stalag Luft I, after his B-26
Marauder was shot down over Italy in July of 1943.

The instant the wheels of the B-17
ahead of him
lifted from the runaway,
Butter pushed the throttles
forward full force.

The Saint
thundered down the runway.

0720 hours.
Liftoff.

Flying straight
for a minute and a half,
Butter then looped to the left
and began a dangerous dance —
spiraling upward 400 feet a minute
and into a "vee"
with two other planes.

Together,
the three planes soared ever higher,
circling once again to allow
a second vee
of three bombers
to pull in behind them.

As Butter kept his hands steady
on the control wheel,
this "squadron" of six planes
slipped into formation
with two other squadrons from the 401st.

Eyes on each plane
kept a sharp lookout for stray aircraft
confused
in the morning's mist.

Few airmen
survived a mid-air collision.

Over the fields of southeastern England,
more than 750 B-17s
and B-24 Liberators
were coiling
into similar formations.

A formation of B-17s from the 309th Bomb Group, based in Nuthampstead, England,
make a bombing run to Neumunster, Germany, on 13 April 1945.

At last,
the Saint and its formation
merged into a bomber stream
that stretched
more than a hundred miles —
its planes all
soaring
east to Berlin.

BERLIN.
The Big B.
Capital of Hitler's "Fortress Europe."

Pre-dawn intelligence reports
had warned
miles and miles of anti-aircraft guns
and some 1500 enemy warplanes
lay in wait to defend
the enemy's largest city.

This mission would be the Allies'
largest daytime strike
on Germany so far.

Trusting their two pilots
not to clip the wing of a nearby plane,
the Saint's gunners squirmed
into battle stations.

Berlin.
What a target
for a new crew
to pull for a second mission.

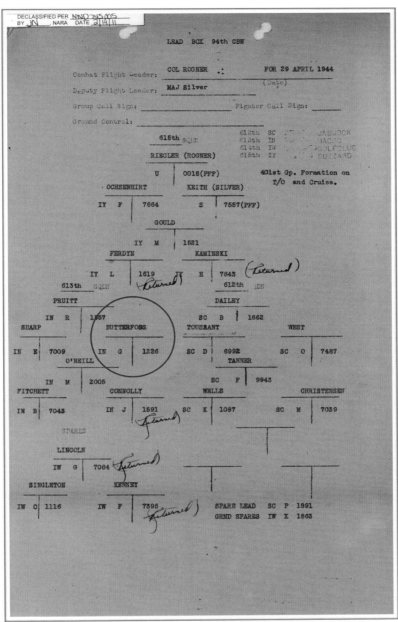

LEAD BOX 94th CBW

Combat Flight Leader: **COL ROGNER** .: **FOR 29 APRIL 1944**

Deputy Flight Leader: **MAJ Silver** (Date)

Group Call Sign: _____ Fighter Call Sign: _____

Ground Control: _____

615th SQDN   612th SC   JASWOOK
              613th IN   MACDO
RIEGLER (ROGNER)   614th IW   GOLFCLUB
              615th IY   BUZZARD

U | 0018(PFF)   401st Gp. Formation on
                      T/O and Cruise.

OCHSENHIRT   KEITH (SILVER)

IY F | 7664   S | 7557(PFF)

GOULD

IY M | 1521

FERDYN   KAMINSKI

IY L | 1619   IY H | 7843 *(Returned)*

613th SQDN *(Returned)*   612th SQDN

PRUITT   DAILEY

IN R | 1357   SC B | 1662

SHARP   BUTTERFOSS   TOUSSANT   WEST

IN E | 7009   IN G | 1226   SC D | 6992   SC O | 7487

O'NEILL   TANNER

IN M | 2005   SC F | 9943

FITCHETT   CONNOLLY   WELLS   CHRISTENSEN

IN B | 7043   IN J | 1591   SC K | 1087   SC M | 7039

(Returned)

SPARES

LINCOLN

IW G | 7084 *(Returned)*

SINGLETON   KENNEY

IW O | 1116   IW F | 7395 *(Returned)*   SPARE LEAD SC P | 1891
                                 GRND SPARES IW X | 1863

Formation assignments for 401st Bomb Group's mission on 29 April 1944.
Each "T" represents 1 plane. 3 squadrons of B-17s took off, along with 3
spares (lower left corner). Planes marked "Returned" had to return to base.
Bombs on the Ferdyn plane were not properly loaded and were jettisoned
over the North Sea. The Connolly plane could not find the formation. The
Kaminski plane had engine trouble and could not keep up with the
formation. Only one spare plane was used. The Singleton plane
moved into Connolly's slot behind the Butterfoss plane.
The two other spares returned to Deenethorpe. [1]

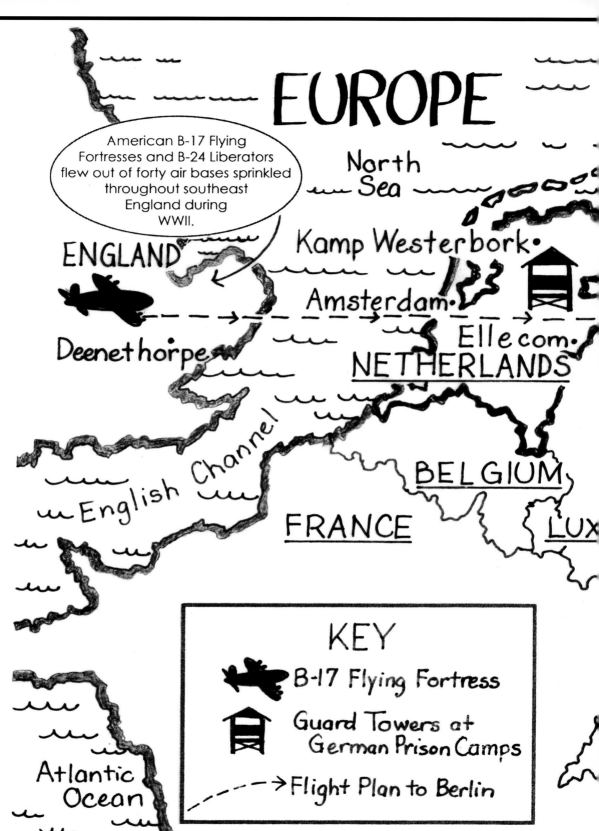

EUROPE

American B-17 Flying Fortresses and B-24 Liberators flew out of forty air bases sprinkled throughout southeast England during WWII.

North Sea

ENGLAND

Kamp Westerbork•

Amsterdam•

Deenethorpe

Ellecom•

NETHERLANDS

English Channel

BELGIUM

FRANCE

LUX

Atlantic Ocean

KEY

B-17 Flying Fortress

Guard Towers at German Prison Camps

→ Flight Plan to Berlin

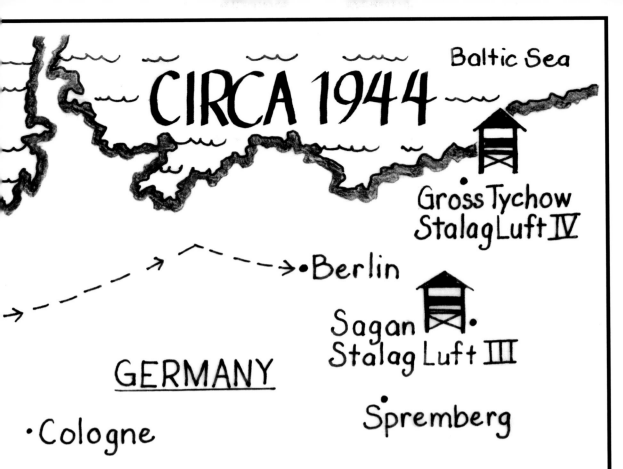

CIRCA 1944

Baltic Sea

Gross Tychow
Stalag Luft IV

Berlin

Sagan
Stalag Luft III

GERMANY

Spremberg

Cologne

Frankfurt

Nuremberg
Stalag Luft XIII-D

Moosburg
Stalag VII-A

N

W   E

S

L. Berry ©

SWITZERLAND

ITALY

* Map not drawn to scale.

Ellecom, Netherlands
29 April 1944
about 08:00 hours

On the top floor
of the large brick house,
behind the gables high above the street,
Joop Levie,
a Dutch *Jood* from nearby Dieren,
pried open sleep-filled eyes.

Jo Gustaaf (Joop) Levie.

The hated walls that had caged him
for more than a year
were still there.

Joop reminded himself…
Be grateful you
and your parents are here —
not crammed into crowded barracks
at Concentratiekamp Vught.
Be happy you no longer have to wear the

Nazis' required yellow star
that makes Jood so easy to identify.

It was difficult, though,
being an *onderduiker*,
someone who went into hiding —
in a cave, a stable, a cellar,
under floorboards,
above a pig sty —
when German raids
began rounding up *Jood*.

He was alive,
but trapped in two rooms
in a house crammed with German soldiers.

He was twenty-one years old.
He should be at university in Rotterdam,
studying banking.
He should be
out strolling in the evenings
with his girlfriend, Willy, on his arm.

He should not be hiding
in his own country,
fearing every minute
black boots would storm up the stairs
and drag him away.

Damn Hitler.
He stole my life.

At least
today was a Saturday.
Downstairs,
the German soldiers —
tall jackboots gleaming with polish
and uniforms brushed clean —
would soon swagger
up the street
and into the Hotel Brinkhorst.

Drunk and stuffed
with chocolate and other foods
the Dutch had not enjoyed for years,
the swine would not return
till well
after midnight.

The Hotel Brinkhorst, owned by Pieter Meijer, was just three doors up the street
from the Bosmans' inn, *Benvenuto*.

The house
could breathe
when the Germans
were gone for the day.
No need to whisper or tip-toe about
for fear the enemy below
would hear.

Bep and Diet
would knock on the door
two times to signal
it was safe to open the door.
Joop and his parents enjoyed
their stories
of life in the village.

The girls were quieter these days —
both worried about
their older sister Nel
and fifteen-year-old brother Jan
who were now *onderduikers* like himself.

The two hid on farms
to avoid German soldiers
who plucked Dutch teenagers and adults
off the streets and shipped them
to Germany
to work
in war factories.

Few had returned home.[2]

Bep and Diet
were safe at home
because they cleaned
and helped their mother cook
when the Germans entertained guests.
Other days,
the pigs took their meals at the hotel.

Left to right: Nel, Bep, Jan, and Diet Bosman, along with Nel's fiancé, Ab Dullemond.

Perhaps today,
Diet and Bep will bring
good news of the war.

Every evening,
Joop had to stop himself
from sneaking down the stairs
to join the Bosmans
in their first-floor sitting room.

He pictured them huddled together.
Bep — who studied English in school —
would be whispering translations
of BBC broadcasts
coming from London
over the hidden radio the German doctor
had allowed them to keep.

Joop especially longed to hear
the brief newscasts
from Queen Wilhelmina
and other Dutch leaders exiled
in London,
that aired at 21:00 hours
on *Radio Oranje*.[3]

Surely,
it is time
Allied ground forces invade
Europe's mainland.

Just survive today,
Joop lectured himself.
Write a letter to Willy.
Diet might have time
to walk
to De Steeg to deliver your letters
and bring Willy's back.

ELLECOM CIRCA 1944

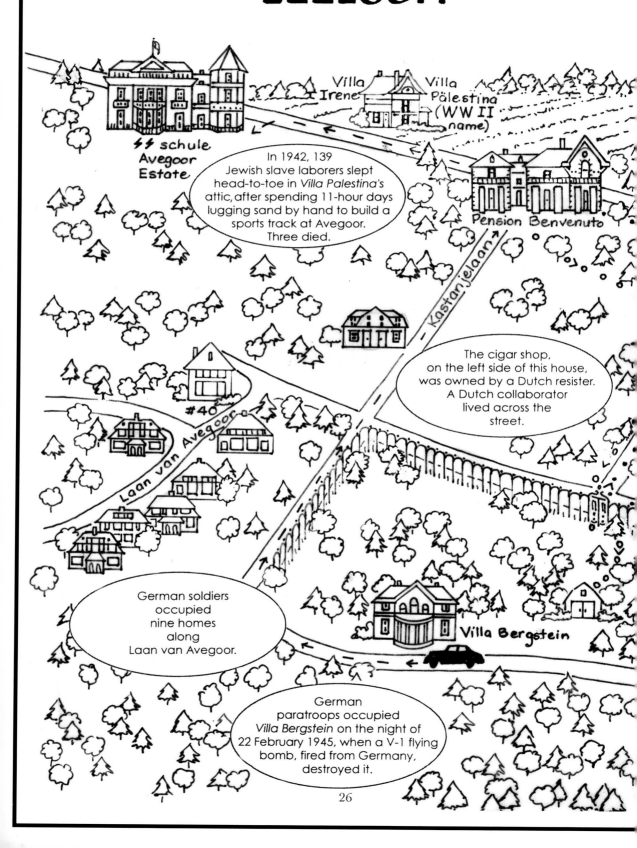

Villa Irene

Villa Palestina (WW II name)

SS schule Avegoor Estate

In 1942, 139 Jewish slave laborers slept head-to-toe in *Villa Palestina's* attic, after spending 11-hour days lugging sand by hand to build a sports track at Avegoor. Three died.

Pension Benvenuto

Kastanjelaan

The cigar shop, on the left side of this house, was owned by a Dutch resister. A Dutch collaborator lived across the street.

#40

Laan van Avegoor

German soldiers occupied nine homes along Laan van Avegoor.

Villa Bergstein

German paratroops occupied *Villa Bergstein* on the night of 22 February 1945, when a V-1 flying bomb, fired from Germany, destroyed it.

NETHERLANDS

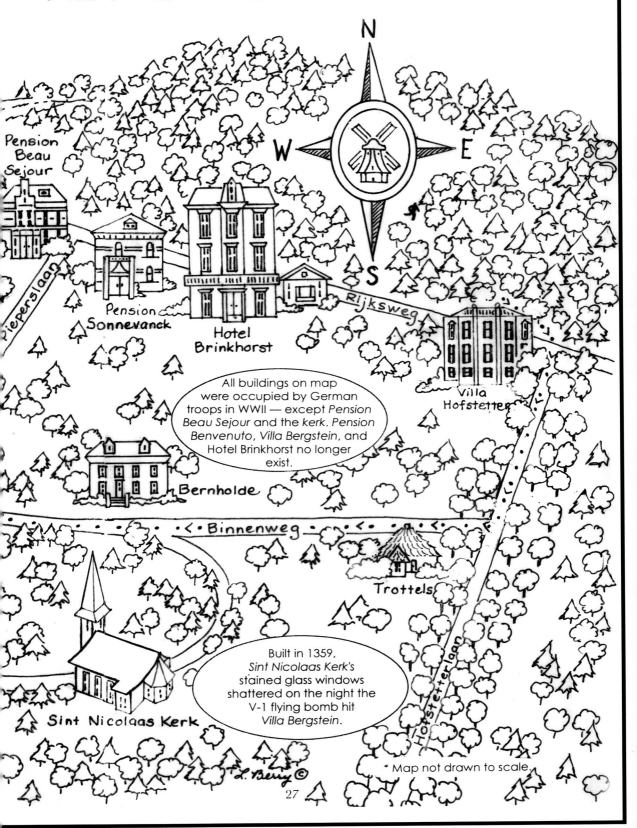

All buildings on map were occupied by German troops in WWII — except *Pension Beau Sejour* and the *kerk*. *Pension Benvenuto*, *Villa Bergstein*, and *Hotel Brinkhorst* no longer exist.

Built in 1359, *Sint Nicolaas Kerk*'s stained glass windows shattered on the night the V-1 flying bomb hit *Villa Bergstein*.

Pension Beau Sejour

Pension Sonnevanck

Hotel Brinkhorst

Villa Hofstetter

Bernholde

Trottels

Sint Nicolaas Kerk

Pieperslaan

Rijksweg

Binnenweg

Hofstetterlaan

* Map not drawn to scale.

L. Berry ©

High over Berlin, Germany
29 April 1944
1140 hours

Dark blobs —
like drops of black paint
splattered on a large blue canvas —
appeared, then disappeared
above the cottony clouds
scuttling
across Berlin.

FLAK.
The dreaded
flying mine fields
that appeared to burst at the whim
of a demented sorcerer.

Black smoke from exploding shells peppers the sky as a formation of
B-17s flies through heavy flak.

Enemy soldiers
fired the exploding shells from
hundreds of German anti-aircraft guns
on the ground far below.

The silent puffs of black smoke
smelled eerily of Fourth of July fireworks
and were harmless.

Not so,
if a bomber was close by
when a fierce red explosion
blasted a shell apart.
A deadly maelstrom of jagged metal
could slash through the plane's thin skin —
crippling engines and slicing
through wiring,
fuel lines,
and human flesh.

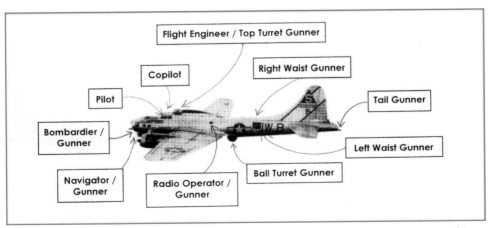

The fire power of a B-17 Flying Fortress came from twelve .50 caliber M2 Browning machine
guns fired by its eight gunners.

Butter and his nine crew members
all knew a direct hit would
send the Saint
screaming
towards earth.

The tight formation,
its planes just fifty feet apart
from one another,
prevented Butter
from dodging the flak.

Draped in steel-lined jackets
and steel helmets for protection,
he and his copilot could only
keep firm hands on the controls,
pray,
and continue the bomb run.

W-H-A-A-M!

Black oil splattered the windshield.
The Saint kicked like an angry bull
on a rampage —
tossing about crew members,
oxygen tanks,
and boxes
of ammunition.

Smoke streamed
from engine one.
Its propeller

spun
out of control.
The stink of gunpowder
and burning oil
flooded the bucking plane.

The pilots clutched
their unruly control wheels,
read the falling gauges,
and worried
the wildly windmilling propeller
on their far left would snap off
and slice
into engine number two.

Butter yelled,
"Cut and feather number one prop."
Both pilots kept an anxious watch
as the spinning propeller
took its time
coming
to
a halt.

"Pilot to crew.
Bad news....
Number one engine is dead.
Number two is at half power.
Good news....
Number one prop is feathered.
There's no fire. No blood.

Wing and tail are mangled pretty bad,
but nothing is falling off.
Target coming up."

As the Saint began
losing altitude and speed,
Butter and his copilot fought
to stay in formation
and hold the plane level.
The two undamaged right engines
kept pulling the plane
to the left.

"Bombardier to pilot.
Flak damaged bomb bay doors.
Opening them manually."

Not one crew member took a breath
till frigid air
gushed
through the aircraft.
Bomb bay doors were open.

"Bombs away."

The B-17
leaped upward,
free of two and a half tons of bombs
now dropping toward
Berlin's
Friedrichstrasse Railroad Station.

A formation of B-17s from the 384th Bomb Group, flying out of Grafton-
Underwood, England, drops its bombs on an enemy target.

Following the flight plan,
Butter made an immediate turn left —
straight
into another flak field.
Falling shrapnel glanced off the plane
as it winged its way westward
to Deenethorpe.

Dropping away
from the protection of the formation,
the slowing fort was now
a straggler —
favorite
prey
of enemy fighter planes.

Eight pairs
of anxious eyes
scanned the sky.

The flight engineer
eyed the falling fuel gauges.
Butter searched for cloud cover.

"Two bandits
closing from the rear."

Butter dove
for the closest cloud.
His bombardier and navigator
grabbed the controls of their machine guns.
The flight engineer
stepped up
into the top gun turret.

All eight gunners held their fire
till the enemy fighters
swooped
closer…
closer…
closer….

ACK-ACK-ACK!
ACK-ACK-ACK!

Ear-splitting racket
of firing machine guns
erupted from all sides
of the
flying fort.

ACK-ACK-ACK!
ACK-ACK-ACK!

Long snakes
of ammunition
fed the Saint's twelve guns.
Brass shell casings
pinged
across its decks.

Silent guns and rowdy cheering
pouring from the interphone
informed the flight deck
two enemy fighters
were spiraling
downward
in
flames.

No one reported
chutes
blossoming
through the smoke.

Butter's job now
was to get his crew home.
It was not the time
to let the fate of two enemy pilots
gnaw at him.
The wounded Saint
had a long way to go.

Ellecom, Netherlands
29 April 1944
12:30 hours

At the back of the large brick house,
far below its attic gables,
steam rose from pots
atop Dien's massive
cast-iron stove.

Heat
radiating
from the black monster
kept the small open-air kitchen
bearable in the
chill of the cloudy day.

Chopping carrots and rutabagas
for the mid-day meal,
Diet and Bep
sat at the worn, wooden table
in the middle of the room.

As Dien stood at the sink
pumping water into a metal pitcher
for the Levies,
her mind drifted away
from her daughters'
chatter.

How she longed
to see Jan's cheerful face.
Please, Lord,
let him get enough to eat
and make him stay out of sight.

She would walk to Drempt
one day soon and check on him.

She missed her oldest daughter as well,
but at least Nel
and her fiancé Ab were
together on his family's farm
outside of Laag Soeren.

Dien worried, too, about Herman.
Her husband did not sleep
at home
most nights.
Rumors that he helped *Jood*
put him in danger of being reported
by Dutch collaborators living in the area.

At this time of day,
he would be pedaling
his wobbly bicycle from farm to farm.
Avoiding German checkpoints.
Searching for whatever
meat and vegetables he could buy —
for his family, the Levies,
and others.

The Germans rationed bread, meat,
sugar, flour, cheese, cooking oil.
Even clothing and shoes.

These ration coupons allowed a family to buy *serviesgoed* — dishes. A family
paid for coupons, used them at a local store to put in an order, then paid the
store owner when the dishes arrived.

Onderduikers
like the Levies
did not dare register
for ration coupons.

Much as Dien worried
about her family,
fear squeezed her heart
whenever she thought of the
van Baarens,
friends of the Levies from Dieren.

Abraham van Baaren,
the village's *Joods* teacher,
his wife Rebekka,

their nineteen-year old son Jacob,
and Rebekka's five-year old nephew
had been *onderduikers*
since last April.

Jacob van Baaren,
circa 1940.

Their hiding place had been
a camouflaged chamber
dug
down
through
the top of a slight hill
deep in the nearby beech forest.

Three young pine trees
stood guard over the hill.

A tailor from Dieren
and two friends
had labored three long nights,
digging the shelter
for the *Joods* family.

The small rectangle on the floor of the hiding place
was a stove.[4]

Quiet as forest hedgehogs,
Diet and Bep had lugged
food and water a mile
to the hole
every two or three nights.

Trails
and lanterns
were too dangerous to use.

With tree stumps
and fallen branches
waiting to trip them in the darkness,
the two had walked with the caution
of high-wire performers.

If they tripped and spilled the water,
it was a long hike home

to pump more.

Despite the risk,
the sisters often climbed
down into the hole
to visit Jacob and his family,
before making their way back
to *Benvenuto*.

One morning in early February,
Germans with guns drawn
had crept
through the woods.

How terrified
the four *onderduikers*
must have been
when enemy machine guns
forced them from the hole.

Where are they?
Are they still alive?

How did the Germans find them?
Who informed on them? [5]

Dien refused to think what
would have happened
if the Germans had raided the hole
while
her girls were visiting.

Forcing a smile
for her daughters,
she went around front to cut tulips.
Tulips to brighten the Levies' tray.
Tulips to hide her hurried peeks
up and down the street.

Wretched Germans were everywhere.
Billeted in many village houses,
they trained
young Dutchmen —
the dreaded blackcoats —
to be *Jood*-hunters at the *SS schule*
on the Avegoor Estate just down the road.

With no enemy uniforms in sight,
Dien climbed the spiral staircase
with the Levies' dinner.

Herman should be along in an hour or so.
And Nel and Ab might walk
through the woods for a visit.

Later,
she would steal
into the doctor's examining room.
A neighbor lady
needed salve
for a nasty skin infection.

High over the Netherlands
29 April 1944
1450 hours

Protective clouds had turned to wisps.
A strong headwind threatened
to push the low-flying B-17
back to Berlin.

Heavy flak jackets, helmets, stools,
oxygen tanks, boxes of ammunition,
even a few guns
had flown
out the bomb bay doors.
Anything to lighten the plane
and save fuel.

"Navigator to pilot.
Land below is now Dutch."

Relief flooded the plane.
Intelligence reports
of infuriated German citizens greeting
downed airmen with pitchforks,
bullets,
and dangling nooses
had preyed on everyone's mind.

Three angry yellow lights, however,
still screamed from the instrument panel.

Each warned
the plane's engines
were running on drops of fuel.

The flight engineer
had banged again and again
on transfer valves in the bomb bay,
but fuel refused
to flow
from the dead engine.

"Bombardier to pilot.
Enemy air base straight ahead.
Bandits scrambling."

CRAP!

Butter punched the alarm button,
then, through its loud clanging,
screamed
over the interphone,
"ABANDON SHIP!"

"ABANDON SHIP!"

Gunners crawled
from ball and tail turrets to clip on chutes.
Bodies tumbled
from hatches
in the rear fuselage
and the open bomb-bay doors.

The radio operator
was still chewing rice paper
scribbled with the mission's code words
when he jumped.
German soldiers were sure to
scour the Saint's wreckage for it.

Crew's out.
Automatic-pilot is on.

With his chute's D-ring clutched
in his right hand
and GI shoes tied around his neck
so they landed with him,
Butter perched on the edge
of the open bomb-bay doors.

The ground was way too close.

If the chute doesn't open in time,
I'm gonna end my days
flatter
than home plate.

Pushing off,
Butter
dropped
from
the
plane.

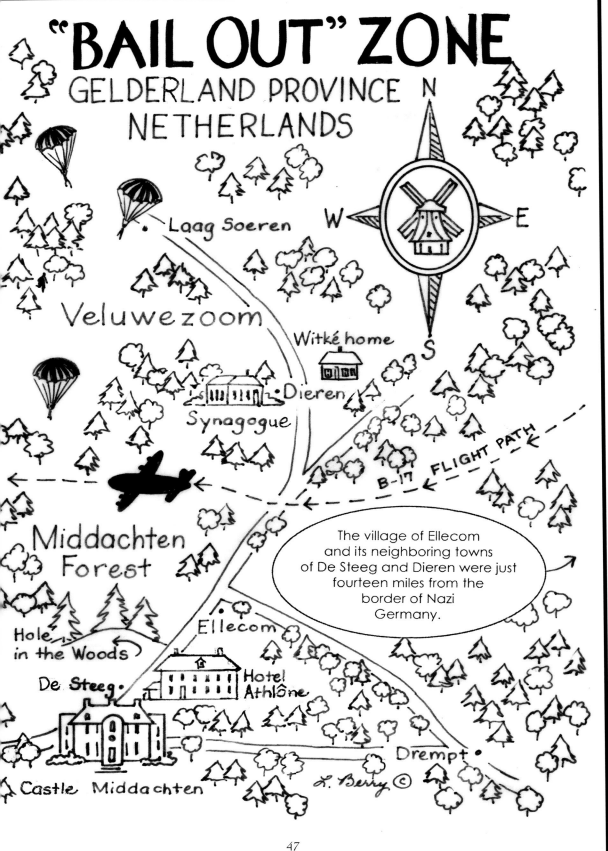

"BAIL OUT" ZONE
GELDERLAND PROVINCE
NETHERLANDS

N

W   E

S

Laag Soeren

Veluwezoom

Witké home

Dieren

Synagogue

FLIGHT PATH

B-17

Middachten Forest

The village of Ellecom and its neighboring towns of De Steeg and Dieren were just fourteen miles from the border of Nazi Germany.

Hole in the Woods

Ellecom

De Steeg

Hotel Athlône

Drempt

Castle Middachten

L. Berry ©

The droning of the
doomed Saint
grew faint.

Twisting about in the air,
Butter recalled
the parachute demonstrator
stressing more than once...
pull the D-ring
when things move on the ground.

Tree branches are swaying ***NOW***.

Butter tugged hard as he could.
The opening chute yanked him upward,
then a blessed canopy ballooned overhead.
No chutes floated below him.
Just tall trees reaching up
to snag him.

Tree landings.
Think about tree landings.

Point
toes
down.
Squeeze legs together.
Press arms against body.
Tilt head
on
shoulder.

Butter ripped
down through a fir tree.
Needles scratched his face.
The smell of Christmas clogged his nose.

His web of silk and cords
snagged on branches,
slowing him
till his toes
grazed
the
ground.

Releasing the chute,
he tied on his government-issued shoes.
Jerked down the parachute.
Buried it
and his clumsy flight boots
under pine needles.

Butter pulled a compass
from a zippered pocket,
then took off
running
in the direction of a village
he had spied from the plane.

Any second
a German motorcycle
would roar through the trees.
He was sure of it.

Do not trip.
Watch out for leaf-filled holes.
Stumps.
Logs.
A twisted ankle or broken leg
will land me
in a prison camp.

Butter ran
through a forest
of towering trees —
each standing straight
as a sergeant at attention.

The national park in which Butter
and his crew landed teemed with
beech and fir trees.

A trickling brook caught his ear.
He knelt to drink for the first time
since breakfast
at 0200 hours.

He almost puked on the horrid taste
caused by purification tablets
from his escape kit.

Standing up,
he was startled to see a face
glaring at him from across the brook.
Not one of his crew,
but an old Dutchman
gripping an axe.

Before Butter could
raise his arms in defense,
the woodsman turned his back
and strode off through the trees.

Taking to his heels,
Butter prayed
the man was not high-tailing it
to the nearest German post to report
seeing an Allied pilot.

Butter ran.
Stumbled.
Walked a bit to catch his breath.
Checked his compass.
Listened
for thrashing boots.
Then ran on
through
the chilly afternoon.

Clouds thickened.
Raindrops
will
mask the sound of running.
None fell.

At long last,
the forest thinned out in front of him.
A dirt trail lay ahead.
Squatting in the brush,
Butter kept watch
on the cobblestone road beyond it.

Blank windows
of a large white house
gaped at him from the other side
of the road.

Exhausted,
Butter devoured two candy bars
he found mashed in a pocket.
Dusk dimmed the sky.
Still no motorcycles.
He marveled at his luck.

Look for ordinary,
everyday people,
an intelligence officer had instructed.
The Dutch have ways
to get pilots back
to England.[6]

At last.
A couple walking
in the gathering gloom.
A couple his age.
They looked
ordinary.

Do it,
or I'll sleep
in this cold, black forest tonight.
*And tomorrow there **WILL** be motorcycles.*
I have to do it now.

With hands up to show
he was not a threat,
Butter
stepped from the bushes
and called in a low voice,
"Please, will you help me?"

The two stopped.
Studied his American uniform.
The young man answered in broken English,
saying they would get help.
His girlfriend set off for the village.

Will she come back with a friend
or German soldiers?

The Dutchman tugged off
his long overcoat and

insisted Butter put it on
over
his dirty uniform.

Plopping his Dutch cap
atop
Butter's
military haircut,
the stranger told Butter
he had seen the low-flying bomber
earlier in the afternoon.
He was pleased to be helping its *piloot*.

The young woman
returned… with another girl.

Phew!

Now
there were
two Dutch couples
out for an evening stroll —
walking
hand-in-hand
into the small village.

Butter barely noticed
the crunch
of gritty black streets
and a tall, pointed church tower
as they sauntered along.

The girl holding his hand
had whispered
German soldiers
and a Dutch collaborator or two
occupied buildings
along the way.

Butter's
eyes darted
from house to house.
He expected to see enemy soldiers
armed with machine guns
in every doorway.

He could tell
the young Dutchman's eyes
were wary of danger,
as well.

Cutting through bushes,
the four approached
the back
of a house.
A large brick house
with windows shuttered
and gables high above their heads. *

* Follow the dots . . . . on the map of Ellecom (p. 26-27) to trace the safest path Nel , Bep, and Ab
   could have walked with Butter to get to *Benvenuto*.

Ellecom, Netherlands
29 April 1944
about 21:00 hours

Dien and Herman greeted the stranger
who walked in
with Bep on his arm.
A man wearing Ab's coat and hat.
An *Amerikaanse piloot* needing help.

Dien pulled
the tense young man
and Bep into the sitting room.
Then shooed Nel and Ab
on their way back
to the safety of Ab's farm.

Diet swept up
leaves
and dirt
from the stranger's shoes,
so the Germans would not be suspicious
when they returned from the hotel.

In the kitchen,
Dien warmed food
for their unexpected guest
while she and Herman debated
what to do.

Helping the *Amerikaanse piloot*
would endanger the Levies' lives
and their own.
They needed to plan
every step with caution.

Herman knew
the Dutch underground
had a network that passed
Allied airmen south through Belgium,
France,
and into neutral Spain.

From there, a boat or plane
could get the young *piloot*
back to England.

Aware he could be shot for
being outside after dark,
Herman stepped into the darkness.
Clouds blocked the stars
like black-out curtains
that hung
in every village window.

Will the password
the German doctor gave me
work if SS soldiers
stop me?

Herman's stomach churned

as he strode down the quiet lane
and knocked two times
on the door of a dark house.
Dien's brother-in-law,
Arend Bos,
was a member
of the Dutch underground.

Back
inside the large brick house,
Dien brought the *Amerikaan*
a tray of meat
and vegetables,
along with bread she had stolen
from the Germans' stash
in the basement.

She spoke rapidly in Dutch.
Bep translated her words
into English
as the young man ate.

Ellecom, Netherlands
29 April 1944
22:00 hours

Step by narrow step,
past the second-floor landing,
Butter followed Bep to the very top
of a winding staircase.
His head spun
with everything she had just explained
about those living
in the large brick house.

HIDDEN JEWS?
GERMAN SOLDIERS?

Somehow,
he had tumbled down
a rabbit hole with Alice
into
a topsy-turvy land swarming
with unseen dangers.

He fought the urge
to dash down
the stairs
and out into the night.

There's nowhere else to go!

Bep first showed him
his small sleeping room
for the night.
Then knocked two times on a door
across the hall.

A Dutchman his age
opened the door and said
in perfect English,
"My name is Joop Levie.
Come in.
This is my father Salomon.
My mother Rosa is asleep."

The three men sat whispering
in the chilly sitting room.
Each kept an ear out
for the thump
of German boots.

WHEN?
Joop demanded.
When would the Allied invasion begin?
Screaming air raid sirens,
blasting flak guns,
and the powerful droning
of hundreds of Allied bombers
filled the Dutch skies
day and night.
But when would ground troops invade?
WHEN?

Soon.
Butter explained British planes
were pounding German cities at night.
American bombers,
flying from both England
and Italy,
were clobbering German airfields,
railways, and factories by day.
All to weaken Hitler's war machine
and the German people's
will to fight.
The invasion was coming.
SOON.
VERY SOON.

Quiet!

What was that?

Nothing.

With his heart skipping beats,
Butter listened to Salomon
speak
of the black day a year ago
when *Jood* of Dieren were ordered to
report to *concentratiekamp Vught*
to await deportation
to *Kamp Westerbork*.

Was that a footstep?

No.

Salomon went on to explain
when Germans first began
rounding up *Jood* three years earlier,
his good friend Herman from bowling club
had two secret sleeping rooms
built
behind sliding doors
under the eaves of his inn's third floor.

Instead
of reporting to Vught,
the three Levies became *onderduikers* —
vanishing
behind the gables
of the large brick house.

It was a terrible shock
to both families
when Germans soldiers strode
into the inn
a few weeks later.

Loud, arrogant voices
had commandeered
two sitting rooms on the first floor
and sleeping rooms on the second.
By sheer luck,
the Germans showed no interest
in the tiny rooms and attics

on the inn's top floor.

The two families learned
to live around the enemy.

Fearing
drunken footsteps
would soon stumble
up the stairs,
the three men shook hands
and wished each other well.

Joop and Salomon
disappeared
into
their sleeping rooms.

Butter tiptoed to his room
across the hall.

Ellecom, Netherlands
30 April 1944
01:00 hours

Beneath the starless sky,
the large brick house
appeared
to sleep
like its neighbors.

That was not so.
In the blackness
of his sleeping room,
Joop twisted his blankets into knots.

Soon.
The invasion would start SOON.
The *piloot* promised.

But will it come in time
to save Jacob?

The hated Green Police —
Dutch civilians
who worked with the Nazis —
had arrested his fun-loving, older brother
in Amsterdam more than a year ago.
Arrested for selling bicycles
when Nazis had forbidden *Jood*
to earn money.

Jacob (Jaap) Levie.

Joop had traveled to Amsterdam
to visit his brother in jail.
When he returned a second time,
Jacob had
disappeared.

Jacob, where are you?

Across the hall,
in a narrow room
with a small, round window,
Butter listened to muffled bumps
coming from below.

GERMANS.

He lay stiff as a propeller blade,
not daring to breathe.
Questions spun through his mind.

No gunshots had shattered the quiet
while he drifted
below his parachute.
He prayed that meant his men
were alive.

Were they sleeping in haystacks?
Under piles of leaves?
In prison cells?

Where would he find himself
tomorrow night?
On his way back to England
or behind a barbed wire fence
of a German prison camp?

It occurred to Butter that this night
he, too, was an *onderduiker*
hunted by the Nazis.

Don't snore.
Don't talk in your sleep.
Don't even turn over.
Any strange noise will bring
Germans pounding up the stairs.

On the floor below,
Dien stared at the ceiling.
Wide awake —

even though Herman had returned
for the night.
She forced herself
to think
of the next day's tasks.

She was to ring her brother-in-law
as soon as the German medical staff
left at midday
to eat at the hotel.
Arend would then come
for the *piloot*.

She needed to steal more coal.

She…

Oh, Dear Lord,
she pleaded.
Please keep German patrols
from raiding this house tonight.

Her family
and the Levies
would be dragged
into the street and shot
if the young *Amerikaan* was discovered.

Dear Lord,
I beg of You….

Ellecom, Netherlands
30 April 1944
04:00 hours

Flickering oil lamps
chased
black shadows
from the chilly kitchen
of the large brick house.

Though grateful
the night had remained quiet,
Dien was still uneasy.

Count each and every German.
Make certain they all leave the house
for their mid-day meal.

Dien reminded herself over and over,
while she made bread filling
for the piloot's breakfast.

Count each
and every German.

She shuddered,
remembering the day
when she thought they would all die
because she had
miscounted.

Diet had been carrying
a tray
heavy with the Levies' food,
when she tripped
on the second floor landing.

Dishes
exploded
like grenades
when they crashed to the floor.

Dien was halfway up the steps to help,
when a sleeping door creaked open.
Her heart stopped
when a German voice demanded,
"What is happening here?"

She was still amazed
the soldier actually believed
Diet's sputtering
explanation about her sister
being sick in bed upstairs.

Glaring at the mess,
the German had mumbled,
"Your sister eats well when she is ill." [7]
Then he clomped down the stairs
and out the door.

Count each
and every German.

Ellecom, Netherlands
30 Apr 1944
12:30 hours

Once again
dressed in a borrowed longcoat
and Dutch cap,
Butter strode through
the Nazi-infested village.

Which front door
is going to open and spew enemy soldiers
into the street?

Alongside him was a stranger,
who had cautioned him
not to speak
if stopped along the way.

Waking early,
Butter hadn't budged
till Mrs. Bosman's double-knock signaled
the German soldiers had left
for the hotel.

Knowing the danger
he had brought the two Dutch families,
he had struggled to tell her
just how grateful
he was for their help.

As he walked,
Butter repeated to himself…
Herman Bosman. Ellecom.
Herman Bosman. Ellecom.
B-O-S-M-A-N.
E-L-L-E-C-O-M.

He would not forget.

Butter felt safer
when the two slipped
through an ornate iron gate
and skirted colorful tulip beds
of an elegant home. *

Butter's guide
ducked into a garage.
There,
a second stranger
from the Dutch underground
crushed his hopes of returning to England
with one word.

"Impossible."

With Hitler expecting
an Allied invasion any day,
piloot escape routes south to Spain
were now too dangerous to use.

* Follow the circles o o o o o o o on the map of Ellecom (p. 26-27) to trace the safest path Butter and the
man from the underground could have taken from *Benvenuto* to *Villa Bergstein.*

71

Every border bristled
with mortars,
tanks,
and extra troops.

Impossible, too, were escapes
in fishing boats across the North Sea.
Mines,
coils of barbed wire,
and machine gun bunkers littered
the Dutch coast.

Butter's spirits
sank further
as the men continued talking.

Returning
to the large brick house
would further endanger
the Bosmans and the Levies.
Remaining
with the underground
was too risky, as well.

The two men believed
surrendering to the *SS* commandant
at Avegoor Estate
was the *Amerikaan's*
only
option.

Villa Bergstein was the home of Mr. and Mrs. Mees, parents of
Madame Wilhelmina de Villeneuve.

Madame de Villeneuve,
who worked for the Red Cross
and was currently staying
in her father's comfortable home,
would call
to arrange Butter's surrender. [8]

Before Butter knew it,
an ominous black car
whisked away
his freedom.
As it sped
from the fenced-in house,
he steeled himself for what lay ahead.

He had been warned what to expect.
Solitary confinement.
Interrogation.

Then incarceration behind
tall wire fences of a remote prison camp.

Name.
Rank.
Serial number.
It was his duty
to state those three facts.
Nothing more.

The car
slowed
as it approached
a castle-like building
with balconies and a tower.

Inspection at *SS schule* on the Avegoor Estate — located on the outskirts of Ellecom.

A huge swastika
flapping above the roof
drove chills through Butter. *

He had
just enough time
to pray
the Bosmans and Levies
would survive the war,
before the car halted.

His door swung open.

A harsh voice barked in broken English,
"For you the war is over." [9]

*Follow the dashes — — — — — on the map of Ellecom (p. 26-27) to trace the streets the German car most
likely traveled when it took Butter from *Villa Bergstein* to the *SS schule* on the Avegoor Estate.

Ellecom, Netherlands
30 April 1944
13:30 hours

The Levies' sitting room
sat tucked under the deep eaves
of the large brick house.

Its furnishings were sparse.
Old-fashioned.
Dusty.
The black heating stove stood cold.

Should Germans kick open the door,
the room would appear unused.
Its sliding doors
into the sleeping rooms were seamless.

Dien
and the Levies
stared at one another
across food growing cold on a tray.

Where is the
Amerikaanse piloot?

They hoped he was already
on his way back to England
to drop more
bombs

on
Hitler.

They also prayed
the young *piloot* was right
about the coming invasion.

*Will we ever learn
what becomes of him?*

Amsterdam, Netherlands
1 May 1944
early evening

CLANK.
CLANK.
CLANK.
CLANK.
CLANK.

In a shadowy corridor,
heavy doors of solitary cells
slammed shut behind Butter
and four of his crew.

Not long after the black car
delivered Butter to the *SS schule*,
his bombardier and navigator had turned up.
Both were as frustrated as Butter
to be in enemy hands.

Earlier this morning,
the three had embarked on a bone-shaking
truck ride to Amsterdam.
Their number swelled to five
when the Saint's co-pilot and tail gunner
climbed in at a town named Arnhem.

Hours later,
the truck had bounced

over cobblestones and bridges
and past the tall canal houses
of Amsterdam.

Canal houses seen from Damrak
Avenue, a major street in Amsterdam
— capital of the Netherlands.

The truck had grounded to a halt
before a grim building.
The flag of the German *Luftwaffe* —
Hitler's air force —
flapped in a chill breeze.

Butter now peered
around his closet of a cell.
It was dim,
damp,
cold.

Fleas hopped
around the only blanket,
as he stretched out on the
narrow, wooden bunk.

Early the next day,
a stone-faced *Luftwaffe* officer —
standing erect
in a crisp blue uniform —
began firing questions at Butter.

Questions about targets,
radar systems,
navigation equipment.

"My name is Donald Earl Butterfoss.
My rank is Second Lieutenant.
My serial number is 0810818."

"My name is Donald Earl Butterfoss.
My rank is Second Lieutenant.
My serial number is 0810818."

Butter's third "My name is…."
unleashed shouts.
Screams.
Threats.

"Prove you are a pilot.
If you can not, we will drag you outside
and —

BANG —
shoot you as a spy."[10]

The steely eyes
of the interrogator
bore into Butter's brain,
daring him to fend off the threats.

Butter's insides
began to quiver.
He narrowed his eyes.
Forced himself to take a deep breath.
Gave himself a talking-to.

You are commander of your crew.
Act like one.

If the two Dutch families.
can live with danger
every hour
of the day,
you can damn well recite
three short sentences over and over.
Then over and over once again.

Taking a deep breath,
Butter glared back
at the German
and —
in a firm voice —
said....

"My name is Donald Earl Butterfoss.
My rank is Second Lieutenant.
My serial number is 0810818."

More days of questions followed.
Along with more threats,
watery tea,
and a few sandwiches of sour margarine
spread on black bread
thin and tasty as cardboard.
Each day ended
with a lengthy scratching bout
with Butter's tiny cellmates.

Then it was over — for the time being.

Rifles prodded
Butter and his three officers
onto a crowded truck —
part of a caravan transporting
American airmen.

As they bounced along,
Butter learned
his radio operator
and two of his gunners
had been spotted in the prison.

The short, jarring trip
ended at an enormous brick building
too grand to be a train station.

Luftwaffe guards,
armed with
long-handled grenades
and rifles with fixed bayonets,
herded the airmen into train cars.

The four crammed
into a small compartment,
followed by a guard brandishing
a machine pistol.

As the steam engine chugged
into the flat Dutch countryside,
Butter took a close look
at his men.
Shook his head.
Despite the danger
they were in, he had to chuckle.

Uniforms were torn.
Caked with filth.
Faces sported scabbed-over scratches
and straggly beginnings of beards.
Grimy hair stuck up
any-which-way.

It was a tossup
as to who
stunk the worst.

Dragging Butter and his men

back to Germany against their will,
train wheels
click-clacked over the rails.
Their guard drew the shades down
to the windowsill
as they crossed the border.

When the German stepped out at Cologne,
all the airmen snuck a peek.

Ruins.
Piles of rubble
as far as they could see.
Allied bombing was demolishing
the city.

Cologne, Germany, 1945. The twin spires of Cologne's cathedral
stared down at a city in ruins.

At the Frankfurt station,
the American airmen stood waiting
for their next train.

No glass remained in the dome overhead.
Fire had charred the walls
pitch-black.

German civilians standing nearby
began muttering.
Louder.
Louder.

Most spoke in German.
A few in English.
Their hate-filled words
were frightening
as a flak field.

"Terror fliegers."
    "Terror flyers."

"Luftgangsters."
    "Air gangsters."

"Mörder."
    "MURDERERS!"

Shaking clenched fists
in the air

and slicing fingers
across their throats,
the hostile crowd edged
towards the captured airmen.

The prisoners were
caught
between the mob
and the *Luftwaffe* guards.

Butter's eyes were scouring
every corner
for possible cover for his men,
when the shuffling feet stopped.

Looking around,
Butter and his crew saw a strange sight.
Luftwaffe rifles were
aiming straight at the hearts
of their own countrymen.

Still
grumbling
and gesturing,
the angry crowd
backed away
from
the prisoners.

Dulag Luft
Transit Camp Air
Oberursel, Germany
mid-May 1944

Butter's heart had stopped pounding
by the time the new train
dropped
the Americans
and their guards
at a quiet station in a German town
called Oberursel.

Dulag Luft —
the *Luftwaffe's*
main interrogation center —
was a short, uneventful march away.

At *Dulag Luft*, Germans held captured Allied airmen in solitary confinement cells
for a period of one to two weeks.

Once more,
a key turned behind him.
Butter stared at his new
cell.

A pail for a latrine.
Another narrow, wooden bed.
A short blanket inhabited by more fleas.
A locked window.
Stifling heat.
And a thick, wooden door
with a keyhole big enough
to swallow a rat.

Early the following morning,
questions
pelted
Butter once again.

"My name is Donald Earl Butterfoss.
My rank is Second Lieutenant.
My serial number is 0810818."

Screeching threats started again.
"We have not yet reported
your capture.
Shooting you is not a problem —
you murder children."[11]

"My name is Donald Earl Butterfoss.
My rank is Second Lieutenant.

My serial number is 0810818."

One interrogator tried a different tactic.
Wearing a Red Cross armband
and a wide smile,
he squeezed
into Butter's cell one afternoon.
Clutched in his hand
was a long,
official-looking form
for Butter to complete.

All the smiling German heard was....

"My name is Donald Earl Butterfoss.
My rank is Second Lieutenant.
My serial number is 0810818."

At long last,
another train deposited
Butter and other Allied airmen
outside the town of Sagan
in mid-May.

Guards marched
the prisoners-of-war
down a gloomy
forest road.
Butter,
his co-pilot,
bombardier, and navigator

stuck together.

Butter worried about
the two waist gunners
no one had
come across in the Amsterdam prison.
He prayed
they had managed to evade
German forces.

Gray clouds hung low.
Sandy gray soil dusted their boots.
Even the straggly pine trees
along the way
were more gray than green.

The pines soon
gave way
to a massive clearing.

Tall barbed-wire fences
and menacing guard towers —
armed with machine guns
and searchlights —
encircled the four,
as the gates of *Stalag Luft III*
clinked
shut.

Each airman
dragged the same

dismal thought
through
the wire gates.

The world
will go on fighting Hitler —
without
me.

Lt. Robert Kerpen, bombardier on The Saint and Ten Sinners, sketched this guard tower while incarcerated at *Stalag Luft III*. He and Butter were both assigned to Barracks 162.

Ellecom, Netherlands
6 June 1944
13:00 hours

The sitting room
of the large brick house
was bursting with joy.
Bep kept forgetting
to whisper as she translated the
BBC's special midday news bulletin.

She wanted to shout
and twirl
around the room.
The Allied invasion promised
by the *Amerikaanse piloot*
had begun.

In the deep blackness before dawn,
thousands of ships had sailed
from England
and now clogged
the English Channel.

Allied soldiers and tanks
were storming French beaches
at Normandy.

Allied bombs blasted
German artillery positions.

Paratroops
rained
down
on the French countryside.

*Is the Amerikaan flying
one of the bombers?*

*How soon will the Allies
free the Netherlands?*

Spotting no Germans out the window,
she and Diet dashed
up the stairs
to tell the Levies.

The Allied Armada coming ashore on Omaha Beach, France,
several days after D-Day.

Stalag Luft III
Prisoner of war Camp Air Three
Sagan, Germany
6 June 1944
1400 hours

Butter stood in a cluster of fellow *kriegies* —

the airmen's smart-alecky version

of *Kriegsgefangenen,*

German

for prisoners of war.

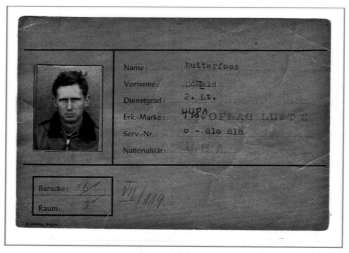

Butter's identification card from *Stalag Luft III.*
A clerk made a mistake typing his first name. He was assigned to
Raum (Room) 22 in *Baracke* (Barracks) 162, West Compound.

A German-speaking *kriegie*

was translating the loud squawking

that had been spilling

from prison loudspeakers for hours.

Weak Allied forces

were attempting
to invade
Hitler's Fortress Europe.
Superior German troops were pushing them
back into the sea with ease.

Butter knew
kriegies would get
the real scoop
soon as it was safe for
senior officers to listen to BBC newscasts
on the few forbidden radios concealed
in hide-holes throughout the camp.

He and his three officers
had been quick to learn that
days in *Stalag Luft III*
were long.
Hot.
Dusty.
Boring.

Playing baseball
with hard-used equipment
from the YMCA
helped fill the dreary hours.
Butter's barracks was determined
to be West Compound's champions.

Learning
to play bridge

also ate up the time.

How his mother
and her bridge club ladies —
in their white gloves and flowered hats —
would gasp in horror
at the stained and faded cards
kriegies dealt one another.

Far more important, though,
four weeks
behind the tall barbed-wire fences
had taught Butter that....

Shattering glass and bodies,
bullets could whiz through windows
if lights were left on
even a minute
after midnight.

Tower guards would
shoot to kill
if he wandered too close
to the "line of death" —
a low wire running thirty feet
inside
the fence line.

Butter also discovered
hunger squirmed
into his bunk every night.

Kriegies walking for exercise kept a careful distance from the low "line of death" wire.

His daily share of Red Cross
tinned meat, powdered milk,
and cheese —
added to the enemy's black bread,
cabbage,
and moldy potatoes —
never chased away
the gnawing in his stomach.

Extra food he got from trading
Red Cross cigarettes
to smokers
only satisfied the snarly beast
for a short while.

His bombardier had come up
with a unique solution
to his growling stomach.

Kerp had spent hours
punching
a hole
in his German-issued spoon,
with a nail liberated
from the frame of his bunk.

Wearing the spoon on a bit of twine
around his neck,
he proclaimed with pride to all
who would listen,
he would never again miss
an opportunity to put food in his mouth.

Lt. Robert Kerpen's spoon survived the war and the
long shipride back to the USA.

Hunger would have been
far worse
if trucks carrying
Red Cross boxes from Switzerland
could not get through
to the camp.

On this warm June day,
Butter and his 10,000 fellow *kriegies*
paid no attention
to boredom,

grumbling stomachs,
and menacing machine guns.

Spirits soared
high
as
white contrails
streaming behind a B-17.

The only frustration tormenting
each prisoner
was that he was not
flying
over France
on this momentous day.

Late that night,
bright searchlights
shredded the inky blackness,
and guard dogs snarled at shadows.

Butter ignored the lumps
of his sawdust-filled mattress,
as thoughts of his fiancée
swirled
through his head.

His men teased him constantly
for being engaged
to a corporal
who wore combat boots.

They could tease all they wanted.
His Helen was, hands down,
the prettiest potato-peeler
in the entire
United States Marine Corps.

And with the Allied invasion
underway at last,
getting home
to hug and kiss her
might be just around the bend.

A troublesome thought
wormed
into his head.

Will invasion forces
reach
tiny Ellecom
before the Germans
discover three onderduikers
hiding above their heads?

Ellecom, Netherlands
18 November 1944
mid-afternoon

In the large brick house,
Salomon sat still as a lump of coal,
peering out
the small, round window
high above the street.

Dien would scold him.
But it was a Saturday.
With the blasted Germans at the hotel,
he'd be safe looking out the window.
It was the only link
to his old life.

Herman had told him
the funeral procession of a close friend
would pass by *Benvenuto* this afternoon.

While Salomon waited,
he thought of all he had seen
from the little window.
Most days,
only a few villagers
or strutting Germans passed below him.

Mid-September,
however,

had brought a flood of families
flowing past his lookout.

For nine, hope-filled days,
the Bosmans and Levies
had listened
to the distant thunder of war
rumbling through the chill
autumn air.

Nine miles to the west,
thousands of British and Polish
paratroops had fought
to grapple
Arnhem's bridge
across the Rhine River
from the Germans.

British, Polish, and American paratroops of the 1st Allied
Airborne Army faced a stronger than expected German
defense around Arnhem, and supporting ground
troops were slowed by narrow roads.

In the midst
of blistering gunfire,
burning buildings, and bloodshed,
the Germans gave
the 100,000 people of Arnhem
twenty-four hours
to evacuate their homes.

Salomon had watched
with dismay
as sobbing children stumbled
along the cobblestones
below him.

Grown-ups plodded in silence,
pushing bundles
and boxes of belongings
piled high atop anything that moved —
bicycles wobbling on bare rims
or wooden wheels,
hand carts,
toy wagons,
baby carriages.

Day after day,
refugees
struggled
past
Salomon's window.

Where would they all find food and shelter?

A refugee family from Arnhem. The metal bicycle wheels were bare because all rubber in the Netherlands went to the German war effort.

The Allies' loss at Arnhem
filled the large brick house with dismay.
Liberation had been so close.
The plight of the refugees,
though,
reminded the Bosmans and Levies
to be grateful they had *Benvenuto.*

Salomon knew Nel still helped
many of the refugees
with medicines
Dien stole
again and again
from the doctor's examining room.

The past few weeks,

however,
Salomon had been encouraged
by the clusters of Dutch blackcoats,
Green Police,
even weary German soldiers
passing below him.
All tromping east
toward the German border.

Good riddance!

He worried about his missing son Jacob,
and the van Baarens.
He worried about the *Amerikaanse piloot,*
who was just months older
than Joop.

The Allies
soon better kick out
the rest of the murdering scum.

At long last,
the funeral procession
reached *Benvenuto.*
With his nose glued to the window
and aching to catch sight of old friends,
Salomon studied
every face.

He never heard
heavy

footsteps
on the stairs
until it was too late to hide.

Searching for suitcases
to stuff full with looted treasures,
two members of the Green Police
had forced their way
into the house.

Shocked to find a *Jood*
peering out a third floor window,
they seized Salomon.
Then scoured
the house for more *onderduikers*.

They were disappointed when they
discovered no other *Jood*.

Bep had had enough time
to knock on the Levies' door.
Her one knock sent Joop and Rosa
scrambling
into the hidden rooms.
Bep hadn't known
Salomon was across the hall.

Clutching
several suitcases,
the Dutch collaborators
shoved Salomon

out the front door
and down the street —
laughing
when he stumbled to his knees.

Late the next day,
Diet and Bep's boyfriend [12]
pedaled
the short distance
to a safe house in Dieren.

Joop and Rosa balanced on the backs
of their bicycles.
Fear perched alongside them.

Worrying about Salomon,
the two *onderduikers*
clung like barnacles
as the bikes bumped along the road.

Where is he?
Oh, Lord,
please guard him
and keep him safe.

Ellecom, Netherlands
25 December 1944
13:00 hours

Frost
coating the sleeping tulip beds
had glittered like cut diamonds
as Christmas Day
dawned
on the large brick house.

The Germans
paraded out early
to feast and drink at the hotel.

Pleased their father was home,
Diet and Bep passed out handmade gifts —
mittens, stockings, and socks
knit from wool
unraveled
from worn-out sweaters.

But Nel and Ab were not there.
Nor were Jan's
mischievous grins.
Empty rooms behind the attic gables
also dampened the sparkle
of Christmas Day.

Listening to the news from the radio

before dinner
only deepened the gloom.
Nine days earlier,
Germany had launched
a fierce attack on Americans lines
in Belgium's
snow-filled Ardennes Forest.

Allied soldiers
were dying this Christmas Day
as the Battle of the Bulge
raged on.

In the western cities
of Amsterdam, Rotterdam,
and The Hague,
people were also dying — from hunger.
Families were forced to eat
tulip bulbs,
toothpaste,
even baked dog.
Chairs, tables, and kitchen cabinets
went up in smoke for heat.

City folk trudged
far into the frozen countryside.
They traded jewelry and other valuables
for a few potatoes.
A bottle of milk.
A handful of eggs.
Anything to survive

what *Radio Oranje* called
de hongerwinter — the hunger winter.[13]

Angry that Dutch rail workers
had shut down the trains
in support of the Allied invasion in the fall,
Germans — in retaliation — refused
to allow food and fuel
into the cities.
And so men, women, and children were dying.

BAM!
BAM!
BAM!

Heavy fists battered the front door
like sledge hammers.

Knowing trouble was knocking,
Dien and Herman
walked slowly
to the door
to give the girls time
to stuff the radio into the cupboard.

A scowling blackcoat
prowled back and forth
on the stoop.
Shoving Herman aside,
he ripped through the attic
and the Bosmans' sleeping rooms.

Belongings
crashed to the floor
in his frantic search for evidence
to prove the *Jood* captured in November
had been living
in the large brick house.

Furious at finding nothing,
the blackcoat hurled threats
at Herman.

He could confiscate all Herman's money.
Take Herman's inn.
Execute Herman
and his family
for daring to hide a *Jood*.

The irate collaborator
then stomped out,
slamming the door behind him.

Fear shattered Christmas.
Herman's face
was pale as the morning's frost.
Dien and the girls stared at their dinner,
unable to lift a spoon.

When will the pounding
come again?

Dieren, Netherlands
31 December 1944
afternoon

B-A-M!
B-A-M!
B-A-M!

This time,
the blackcoat's heavy fists
pummeled the door of the sisters Witké,
who lived next door to the Levies' store.[14]

In the attic,
terror gripped Rosa and Joop.
There was no secret hiding room.

Chaotic shouting shook the house.
The two grabbed coats, hats, blankets —
anything warm —
before they were
marched to the police station.

Early the next morning,
Joop,
Rosa,
and several other
captured *onderduikers*
shivered and straggled
along the cobblestones to Arnhem.

Two old policemen prodded them along.

Near De Steeg,
where Willy lived
in her father's hotel,
bare beech trees marched
in double lines along the road.

Beyond the trees,
a deep ditch twisted
through tall dried weeds.

Lost in misery,
Rosa was startled when Joop
pulled her close and whispered,
"Do not fret about me,
Mother."

Lagging behind her,
he slipped
into the frost-filled ditch
and squiggled toward the thick forest.

Rosa wanted to scream.

I am alone.
I can't survive
this horror by myself.
I can't do it alone.
But
if I scream,

shots will ring out.
Joop will die.

She would not lose Joop that way.
She willed herself
to stay silent.
Willed herself to not look back.

Jacob disappeared
while in the hands
of the police.
It is safer that Joop escapes now.

When the policemen discovered
they were one prisoner short,
Rosa played dumb.
Kept a blank look
on her face
as she trudged to Arnhem.

That look
accompanied her on a truck ride
north to the barbed-wire gates
of *Kamp Westerbork*.

Rosa stared
at watch towers.
Guards strutting about
with machine guns.
Flat fields
beyond tall wire fences.

A deep ditch dug by prisoners lay between the barbed wire fence and the barracks at *Kamp Westerbork*.

Frigid winds
flung sandy soil in her face
and gnawed
through her coat.

Rosa had heard whispers about
Westerbork.
A place where *Jood* waited
to board trains leaving
for labor camps
in the east.

A place
from which no one

had yet returned.

After guards searched her
and filled out forms,
Rosa set off
along the *Boulevard des Misères*
to find the women's barracks.

What a frightful name
for a street.
What happens in this place?

Dilapidated barracks stood empty.
On a deserted playground,
teeter-totters pointed to the sky.
Swings
swung
alone
in the wind.

Does Rebekka van Baaren
push her small nephew
on one?

The commandant's
green and white
house looked out of place —
like a vacation home
in a sea of gray barracks.

"Rosa?"

"ROSA?"

She turned in shock.
Salomon?
It was Salomon.
He was thinner, dirty, weary.
A toddling old man,
who seemed lost in the prison.
None of that mattered.
He was there.

Is Jacob here, too?
The van Baarens?

Salomon's head
drooped
with sorrow.

Less than 900 *Jood*
and others were still there.
Hitler had stopped the trains to Poland
in September,
when Allied troops
began pushing into the Netherlands.

Clinging to her,
Salomon pointed to train rails
stretching eastward.
Rosa stared down the tracks
their older son must have
traveled.

Traveled where?
To a labor camp
or to some unimaginable hell?

NO.

Jacob is sturdy.
Joop is smart.
They will come home
at the end of this insanity.
They will both come home.

Paper-thin slices of black bread
made with more sawdust
than grain.
Slimy, boiled cabbage.
A small mouthful of potato.

Her first meal at *Kamp Westerbork*
convinced Rosa
she and Salomon
both needed more food
if they were to welcome their sons
back home after the war.

She thought
of the frost-covered fields
outside the wire fences.

Last fall,
prisoners dug potatoes out of those fields.

They might have missed tiny ones.

Rosa watched.
Asked cautious questions.
Was determined to find food.

Several days later,
bitter winds whipped her face,
as she walked across a field.
Guards hadn't stop her
from going out the gate for a walk.

Salomon had told her
escaping wasn't a problem
at Westerbork.
Every inmate understood
if they were not at evening count,
families or bunkmates would suffer.

Stooping over
as if to tie her shoe,
Rosa slipped a small potato
into the pocket of her baggy coat.

Dien Bosman steals
coal and medicine
from under the noses of the Germans.
Rosa Levie now smuggles
vegetables
past
the frozen snouts of Dutch swine.

**On the road to
Spremberg, Germany
28 January 1945
0500 hours**

Butter's thin body shook in the frigid darkness.
Clutching his worn blankets tighter,
he ducked his head
against stinging snow pellets
flung about by wailing winds.

One foot. Then the other.
One numb foot. Then the other.

Word had blown like a hurricane
through *Stalag Luft III*
the previous evening.
Prisoners
had one hour
to stuff belongings into packs
and prepare to march.

Butter's West Compound
had been second out the gates
at 2400 hours.

He had been slogging
through a blizzard
for five hours.

Most *kriegies* carried their meager belongings in blanket rolls slung over their shoulders.
Some airmen dragged sleds, made from benches or small tables.

One foot. Then the other.
One numb foot.

Then the other.

Despite the rotten weather,
ten thousand *kriegies*
were surprised to be alive.

As Russian guns rumbled
closer and closer to the camp,
most had feared Hitler would order
camp guards
to turn
machine guns and rifles on them.

Six.
Seven.
Eight hours dragged by.

Dawn struggled to brighten the sky.
Stark, black trees,
quaint villages,
burned-out barns
appeared, then *poof!* —
disappeared into the relentless snow.

Booming Russian artillery
played
an angry duet
with the savage wind.

Kriegies — who had been
on half-rations for three months —
began floundering.
Heavy packs dropped
into snowdrifts.

Then men.

One
foot.
Then

the....

Butter stopped.

He didn't move.
Couldn't move.

He thought of his parents.
His fiancée Helen.
He thought about the devil
his sister would give him
if he fell out of line.

The blocks of ice attached
to his legs
still refused to move.

Snow.
Wind.
Kriegies.
All swirled past his frosted eyelids.

Then a hand —
strong as Superman's —
reached through the whiteness.
Gripped his elbow.
Pressured him forward.

A slow Texas drawl filled his ear.
Encouraged him.
Bullied him.
Cursed him with words
Butter's sister
didn't
even know.

One

foot.
Then the other.
One numb foot. Then the other.

The strength of a Texan stranger.
Red Cross cigarettes swapped
with German villagers for bread and beer.
A few hours of sleep caught
on the crowded floor
of a warm pottery factory.
More shuteye in barns and churches.

All got Butter through the six-day,
fifty-six-mile trek
to freight yards outside
a town named Spremberg.

Guards herded 50
or more prisoners
into each windowless boxcar.
Butter cringed as a vile-smelling pail —
their only latrine —
passed over his head on its way
to a *kriegie* miserable with diarrhea.

The airmen had little food and water.
No medicine.
And not a clue
where the steam engine was headed.

Hotel de Valkenberg
Rheden, Netherlands
February 1945
late evening

Joop squirmed on his bed of straw.
The wool blanket tucked around him
was not thick
enough
to keep cold night air
from torturing him.

Horses no longer
filled the stalls of the *paardestal,*
the stable belonging to the stately
Hotel de Valkenberg.

The horse stalls in the *paardestal* were located in the
wings on either side of the stable.

The German army
had confiscated
horses

early in the war,
but Joop still caught
the lingering odor of manure.

Because the stable nestled in the woods
far from where the elegant hotel
perched on its hilltop,
he felt safe
in the attic space
beneath the peaked roof.

Shivering in the frosty night,
he remembered
the shock
on Willy's face,
when he had turned up
at her father's hotel in De Steeg.

Caked with muck
and bits of brittle, dead leaves,
Joop had known
he couldn't stay long.

Willy's father also realized
heavy fists would soon pound
on the hotel's door.
Over the next few weeks,
he moved Joop to another hotel
and then another —
until Joop felt he was a piece
in a deadly game of chess.

What was that?

Joop held his breath.
Listened.
Someone was moving
near the stalls below.

He stared
into the blackness.
There was no hidden room.
Hands were his only weapons.

"Joop?"

The whisper came again.

"Joop?"

It was Willy's father.

Taking the stairs two-by-two,
he gathered up Joop's few belongings
without a word,
then scattered the straw
across
the floor.
He gestured
for Joop to follow him.

Down the stairs
and out into the winter's night

they went.
Not stopping
until they traveled a far distance
through the frosty forest.

Joop's heart
was still pounding,
when they paused in the shelter
of a cluster of fir trees.

Willy's father whispered
he had learned the butcher
who delivered meat to the hotel
was not to be trusted.
His in-laws
were
collaborators.

The two men then continued on
through the silent trees.

As he tried to avoid stumbling
over downed branches,
Joop wondered
where
he would be hiding
when the sun peeked up
in a few short hours.

Stalag Luft XIII-D
Nuremberg, Germany
26 February 1945
1830 hours

BOOM!

KA-BOOM-BOOM!

BOOM!

Burning buildings tinged the dark sky
with a reddish glow.
Smoke stung weary eyes.
British bombers roared overhead.
Exploding bombs shook the ground.
Air-raid sirens screeched over
the constant

ACK! ACK! ACK!

of enemy anti-aircraft guns.

Butter would have sworn
he was in Hell,
if the dirt beneath his skinny buttocks
had not been cold
as the floor of an igloo.

Wrapped in blankets,
he sat in a crowded slit trench
he had helped
dig

with a tin can.
Bony elbows jabbed his ribs
from both sides.

A paper pillow stuffed with paper shreds
perched atop Butter's head —
his only protection
from flak and bomb fragments
falling
like
heavy
metallic
hailstones.

When Butter and his fellow airmen
had pried themselves
out of foul-smelling boxcars
several weeks earlier,
it didn't take them long to discover
the joys of Nuremberg.

Floors.
Bunks.
Pit latrines.
All wore a thick, crusty coat of filth.

Fleas and lice,
rats, mice, and bedbugs
outnumbered *kriegies*
by the millions.

Kriegies slept
on bare wooden bunks, table tops.
Even on cracked floors
from which
vermin crawled
in the black of night.

Worse of all,
trucks crammed with Red Cross boxes
traveling from Switzerland
found it impossible
to find
their way around
ever-changing battle lines.

Butter and his men
dined on slivers of sawdust bread
and Green Death Soup —
a tasty concoction
of rotting dehydrated vegetables
with maggots
thrown in for protein.

Kriegies soon forgot
rodents and aching stomachs
when Allied planes began pounding
Nuremberg day and night —
hell-bent
on blasting the city
to blackened
rubble.

Hidden radios reported
Yankee tanks closing from the west.
Russian tanks rumbled even closer
from the east.

Butter prayed
one or the other would roll into camp —
PRONTO.

Please, Lord,
before we kriegies are blown
to smithereens
by our own
bombs.

KER-BOOOOM!
BOOOOM!

BOOM!

Kamp Westerbork
Hooghalen, Netherlands
11 April 1945
Morning

Rosa dragged her eyes
open,
hoping it would not be
another blustery, colorless day.
Another day filled
with
nothingness.

She prayed yesterday's
frantic bustle —
German soldiers stuffing
train cars
with
furniture and clothes,
squealing pigs, bellowing cows,
crates of food, clinking bottles of wine —
meant Allied liberators were nearby.

Outside,
in air that still
had a wintry bite,
she found Salomon shuffling
toward her
from the men's barracks.

Rosa smiled.
The smuggled vegetables
were keeping him alive.

The two looked around,
catching sight of the hated Dutch guards
here and about the compound.
None watched
the prisoners.
None seemed to care if jobs got done.

She and Salomon
joined others drifting
up and down the *Boulevard des Misères*
in the ever-blowing wind.

Many were curious
about the guards' behavior.
Consumed by memories
of those sent east,
others stared down train rails,

Rosa and Salomon wandered.
Both sensed the day's
strangeness.

Footsteps
shuffled up behind them.
The two turned
and looked into faces
grubby and gaunt as their own.

A wisp of words
floated
towards them...

"They're gone."

Soft words —
as though a louder voice
might spook
the miraculous happening
into vanishing like a desert mirage.

Another inmate spoke
with more force,
"Guards are gone!"

Rosa and Salomon peered around.
Watch towers stood empty.
Guards were
nowhere to be seen.

Is it a trick?
Can the enemy truly be gone?

Hopeful faces
milled about Westerbork.
All tried to absorb
the fact
Germans and their Dutch helpers
had snuck away
like cowards.

By day's end,
a few had ventured outside the gate.
None dared to walk away
and not come back.
Others delighted in candies
discovered in the deserted camp store.

That night,
Rosa, Salomon, and the rest
fed themselves
what food they could find.
Crawled onto hard iron bunks.
Pulled up flea-infested blankets.

Will we still be free
come daybreak?

At 15:30 the next afternoon,
Canadian armored carriers —
each displaying
a maple leaf with pride —
rolled up
to Westerbork's gates.

The news spread faster
than lice.

The *Boulevard of Misèries*
rang with cheers
and laughter.

A mob of thin, dirty,
delighted prisoners surrounded
the soldiers of the 2nd Canadian Division.
Smothered them with giggles,
hugs,
and questions — most
in a language the soldiers
did not understand.

Crying and laughing,
Rosa and Salomon joined in singing
"Het Wilhelmus,"
their national anthem.
An enormous Dutch flag
and a smaller orange one
unfurled above
the abandoned *SS* headquarters.

Who had been hiding those?

Prisoners
shared candies
with the liberators,
who began a song of their own.
Most of the camp's inmates only understood
its first two words —
"O Canada...."

That night,
iron bunks were still hard.
Fleas and lice still crawled and bit.

Dinner, too,
had been much the same.

Canadian soldiers had been eager
to share their rations
of canned corned beef and peaches,
biscuits, jam, and chocolate.
But officers worried
prisoners' stomachs
could not handle rich food yet.

Smoke from Canadian cigarettes,
however,
spiraled up to the ceiling
in every barracks.

In the dark,
Dutch tongues twisted
around a strange new word.
"Sa - skat - chew - an."
"Saskatchewan."

The Canadian soldiers
came a far way to liberate us.

Rosa and Salomon
both fell asleep that night
with one thought
in their minds.

Are Joop and Jacob free yet?

De Steeg, Netherlands
16 April 1945
07:00 hours

Another hotel.
Another attic.

Joop stared out the dusty window.
Fresh green haze of spring leaves
filled his eyes.

Nothing.

He had been hiding
atop
the Hotel Athlône
for two weeks now.

The Hotel Athlône in De Steeg

He wrote often to Willy.

But thoughts of his family
badgered him
through the long, empty hours
of each day.

Where are they?
Are they all still alive?

Again, he glanced out at the forest.

Nothing!
How can there be nothing after yesterday?

Yesterday,
the silence had
e x p l o d e d
with a **BOOM!**
Then
BOOM! BOOM! BOOM!

Windows rattled.
Shouts and cries carried up
to the attic.

Yet no one
seemed to be hurt.
Black smoke had not billowed
through the bit of sky
he could see.
He couldn't catch a whiff
of anything burning.

If tank artillery
or a German V-1 rocket had hit the hotel,
he would be buried under rubble.

He had passed the night's long hours
tossing in the darkness.
Dawn had brought
a friend of Willy's father,
who delivered his day's food and water.
And information.

In a desperate attempt
to slow down
advancing Allied forces,
German soldiers had dynamited
the double rows of towering beech trees
that arched over the road
between Ellecom and De Steeg.

After blowing up the trees, Germans then booby-trapped the fallen timber
with mines. Several days later, two Canadian solders died while
trying to clear the road with heavy military vehicles.

Trees along the lane
leading to Castle Middachten
had toppled as well.

While Joop ate,
the resistor had stiffled his laughter.
Trees did indeed blocked the road —
looking like a giant's game
of pick-up-sticks.

But in their haste,
German soldiers
had placed dynamite
on the wrong side of many trees.

Those trees now
lay in meadows —
accomplishing nothing more
than confusing
grazing sheep.

The sound of voices reached the attic.

Joop darted to the window.
Below him,
soldiers
poured through the trees.

Canadian soldiers!
LIBERATORS!

With a broad smile on his face,
Joop
bounded
down the stairs
and into the fresh spring air.
He was **FREE!**

Is Jacob free?
Mother?
Father?

Willy's father will be here soon.[15]
He promised we'd start searching
when the Canadians came.

We'll start looking in Dieren.
Today.

Stalag VII-A
Prisoner of war Camp Seven-A
Moosburg, Germany
29 April 1945
1200 hours

Butter hugged the ground.
His nose breathed dust.
Bullets
and heavier artillery shells
had been zipping back and forth
over his head for three hours.

Lord,
this is not the time
for a stray bullet
to have my name on it.

The Yanks are here!
*They are **HERE!***

The news had traveled
faster than a V-1 rocket
through the more than 120,000 Allied
soldiers,
sailors,
marines,
and airmen
now taking cover
in the massive camp.

144

Outside the main gate,
American troops
and tanks
were trading shots with
stubborn *SS* tanks hiding behind
a high railroad embankment
on the far side of camp.

The guard tower at the main
gate of *Stalag VII-A.*

While bullets whizzed
over his head like demonic wasps,
Butter thought
about the journey
he and his men had taken
from the rubble of Nuremberg.

Thank God,
boxes of food from Argentina
and Red Cross packages

from Great Britain and the United States
had shown up a month before orders
sent them marching
once again.

Otherwise,
he and thousands
of other hungry *kriegies*
would have been too weak
to make the soggy hundred-mile,
ten-day hike
to Moosburg.

Rotten luck had struck
the first day of the rainy march.
American fighter planes dive-bombing
a railroad yard
had come too close to a road
crowded with the beginning
of an endless line of trudging *kriegies*.

Three died.
Two Americans and a Brit.

It wasn't fair —
so close to this spring day.

Caked with mud from head to toe,
Butter's crew had straggled
into this monstrous pigsty
two weeks ago.

Allied servicemen
from five continents crammed every inch
of the the wooden barracks
and dirty white tents —
each big enough to house a
traveling circus.

In each tent, 300 captured Allied servicemen snored shoulder to shoulder
on the hard ground.

Worn blankets—
propped up
with blackened boards
rescued
from cook fires —
had served as wobbly shelters
for Butter
and his men.

The four had spent
the past two weeks searching
for the rest of their crew.

They pepper other *kriegies*
with questions.
Stuck noses
through barbed wire
to quiz prisoners in neighboring compounds.
Not a whiff of information
did they uncover.

The shooting dwindled.
Stopped.

A low wave of sound
came at Butter from the direction
of the main gates.
It grew closer.
Louder.

The wave swept the camp
till Butter
and 120,000 other Allies
CHEERED
as one.

Cheered.
Cried.
Jumped with joy.

Screamed to the heavens.
Knelt down and prayed.

Prayed in English,
Polish, French, Italian,
Dutch.
Russian,
and other languages Butter
had never heard.

Jubilant Allied servicemen crowd around the first American tank to plow
through Moosburg's barbed wire fencing.

No longer *kriegies*,
Allied servicemen climbed fences,
poles,
the wobbly walls

of barracks and latrines.

All stretched
their necks to catch sight
of American tanks,
troops,
and the
Stars and Stripes
as it rose high overhead.

Butter and his tent mates
could barely make out the flag.
But tear-filled eyes knew
it was there.

FREE!
Can it really be true?

The war wasn't over yet,
but
Butter and three of his crew
were going
home.

Where
the Sam Hill
are the rest of them?

The Stars and Stripes rose triumphantly over Moosburg
at 1240 hours on 29 April 1945 — one year to the day
Butter and his crew bailed out of their flying fort.

Ellecom, Netherlands
5 May 1945
mid-morning

Front doors swung open.
For the first time in five years,
no dangers lurked
outside.
The folk of Ellecom walked
the streets and lanes,
chattering
and laughing with one another.

German General Johann Blaskowitz,
commander of German troops
in the Netherlands,
was to surrender to the Canadians
in the city of Wageningen.
TODAY!

Smiling,
the Bosmans
walked among friends
and neighbors.

There was much to celebrate.
Hitler had committed suicide five days earlier.
Germany was expected to formally
surrender
in a day or two.

Jan was back home.
Nel and Ab visited often.

Benvenuto was once again theirs.
German medics had squeezed
into a dusty black car that
arrived to collect them
in the nick of time.
Canadian and British troops
rolled into Ellecom
the next day.

Dieren was liberated on 16 April 1945 — the same day as De Steeg and Ellecom.
British soldiers of the 49th Polar Bear Division stand behind joyful villagers.

In mid-step,
Dien and Herman froze.
The Levies
were walking straight at them.
They were ALIVE!

Amid hugs and tears,
handshakes and wide smiles,
the Bosmans peppered them
with questions.

"You are under arrest."
The loud words sliced
through the day's happiness.
The blackcoat from down the street
grabbed at Herman.
Screeched,
"You are under arrest
for helping *Jood* and Allied airmen."

Dien tried to help her husband,
but the blackcoat
was too strong.
Salomon and Joop got a firm grip
on the crazed man at last,
and with the help of others,
forced him out of the neighborhood.

Late that night,
Dien lay awake in bed.
War raged in the Pacific.

Jacob Levie, the van Baarens,
and too many others were still missing.
Reports of death camps were horrifying.
The *Amerikaanse piloot's* fate
was unknown.
And what could be done about blackcoats?

Those were tomorrow's worries.
This night she would sleep
with Queen Wilhelmina's words
in her heart.

"Eindelijk zijn wij weer baas
op eigen erf en in eigen haard."[16]
"At last,
we are in charge
of our own land and homes once more."

As Dien fell asleep,
quiet settled
around the large brick house
and its colorful gardens
of blooming tulips.

The small, round window
high above the street
reflected lights
of a village
no longer smothered
in
blackness.

AFTER THE WAR

Hearts filled with sorrow
when the Levies and Bosmans learned
that Jacob Levie, Rebekka van Baaren,
and Abraham van Baaren had all perished
at Auschwitz Death Camp
in Nazi-held Poland.[17]

Rebekka van Baaren at the
waterwagon in Dieren —
before April 1943.

Jacob van Baaren
and Rebekka's young nephew
also died — most likely at Auschwitz.

Joop graduated
from Erasmas University
in Rotterdam.
He convinced Salomon
to expand De Magneet,
the family's clothing store in Dieren.
Rosa was their best saleswoman.

Rosa Levie.   Salomon Levie.

Two weeks after returning stateside
in early June,
Butter married Corporal Helen Best
of the United States Women's Marine Corps.
Lt. Robert Kerpen, the Saint's bombardier,
served as an usher.

The rest of the B-17's crew
returned home in one piece.
The Germans had incarcerated
five of Butter's crew members
in Stalag Luft IV.
Only the left waist gunner —
Sgt. William Watkins —
managed to evade the enemy
till the end of the war.

Nel and Ab
remained close by,
helping to run his family's farm in Laag-Soeren.
Ab also opened a bakery
in Dieren.
They married on 20 February 1950.

Dien, Herman,
Bep, Diet, and Jan
once again welcomed visitors
to the large brick house
with gables high above the street
and gardens
of tall bright tulips.

The Bosmans sold *Benvenuto* in 1963.
It was torn down in 1978.

On February 15, 1979,
Yad Vashem —
the Holocaust Martyrs' and Heroes'
Remembrance Authority in Israel —
recognized Herman Bosman
and his wife, Dien Bosman-Broers,
as Righteous Among the Nations
for hiding the Levies.

Dien and Herman Bosman in their sitting room at *Benvenuto*.

Flemington, New Jersey
USA
circa 1958

The little girl
with hair straight as a ruler
grew up with two pesty brothers
in a small brick house.

Tall bright tulips
bloomed
in its garden every spring.
Tulips from bulbs sent
by the nice Dutch family.

The little girl grew taller and taller,
but Daddy would still not
tell her about war.

He never did.

But her great-aunt Geri did.
Sitting on a wobbly, wooden chair,
the girl sipped cocoa
in her aunt's old house atop the hill
on Maple Avenue
and listened
to her father's story at last.

German fighter planes?

Parachuting from a dying plane?

The gentle father she knew
never even swore —
well,
except at Christmas time
when she and her brothers
always knocked over the tree.

Prison camps? Interrogations?

As the girl learned more
about World War II
and the Holocaust in high school
and college,
she began to understand
why her father had refused
to tell her about the war long ago.

She had been too young
to learn about such horrors.

She also grew
to realize
that her father
needed to put the war's
bad memories behind him.

The girl knew, though,
her father's story would always be
a part of her.

DEDICATIONS

Diet Geerlings-Bosman
—
For the courage she and her family
showed in World War II
and
for her graciousness
in sharing her memories.

Donald Earl Butterfoss
—
For his service to his country
and for an intriguing story his
great-grandsons Drew Mackneer, Ryan Mackneer,
Lincoln Dobmeier, and Chase Butterfoss
will grow up knowing.

GLOSSARY, BIBLIOGRAPHY, NOTES & OTHER GOOD STUFF

This poster welcomed Allied soldiers to a grateful Netherlands.

GLOSSARY

2Lt. Abbreviation for 2nd lieutenant in the US Army Air Corps.

Allied Powers The United States, United Kingdom, Canada, Australia, New Zealand, South Africa, Soviet Union, and China were fighting the **Axis Powers** — Germany, Japan, and Italy.

Amerikaan Dutch noun for a person from the U.S.A.

Amerikaanse Dutch adjective describing something from the U.S.A.

Army Air Corps The aviation branch of the US military from 1926 to 1941, when it became the Army Air Forces. Military aviation remained part of the US Army until 1947.

BBC British Broadcast Company, a radio station broadcasting from London, England.

bandit German fighter plane on the attack.

bomber stream Entire line of bombers flying towards a target.

Bombardment Group In WWII, the US 8th Air Force was divided into bombardment groups, each with a base in England. Term is often shortened to Bomb Group or BG.

Bombardment Squadron Most Bombardment Groups consisted of four bombardment squadrons. Term is often shortened to Bomb Squad or BS.

chute Short for parachute.

circa About or approximately — used with a date.

collaborator A Dutch traitor who voluntarily helped the Germans.

concentratiekamp Dutch for concentration camp.

deck Flooring of an airplane.

eaves Under the sloping part of a roof where it meets the house walls.

feathering Turning a wildly-spinning propeller into the wind to stop it.

flak Exploding shells from an antiaircraft gun. German term for this type of gun was *flieger abwehr kanone*. The term flak was created from the underlined letters.

flak jacket Canvas coat lined with 30 pounds of steel plates — worn to protect airmen from metal shards of exploding shells.

flight deck Cockpit of plane — pilot sat on left and copilot on right, with flight engineer/top turret gunner just behind them.

Fortress Europe Nazi Germany and all its occupied territory.

fuselage Main body of a plane.

gable Pointed part of a house wall formed by the roof's slope.

GI Abbreviation for Government Issued. Regular GI army boots and GI shoes were better for running than soft flight boots.

goose-stepping Marching with legs held straight and swinging high.

hardstands Round, paved parking spots for Allied planes.

headwind Wind blowing directly at the nose of a plane.

Holocaust In an attempt to rid Europe of all Jews, Hitler's Nazis killed almost six million Jews in their death camps. Five million non-Jewish civilians also perished in the camps.

interphone Intercom. A B-17 crew member was connected to the plane's interphone by a throat microphone and earphones.

jettison To deliberately dump something from a plane or ship.

kerk Dutch for church.

Jood Dutch for person(s) of the Jewish religion. *Joods* means Jewish.

latrine A toilet — usually a common one in a camp or barracks.

maelstrom A violent, swirling chaos — comes from the 17th century Dutch word *maalstrom*.

medallion Small, religious medal on a chain worn around the neck.

onderduiker Dutch for person in hiding from Nazis.

pension Dutch for inn.

piloot Dutch for pilot.

poop Slang for important information.

POW Abbreviation for prisoner of war.

RAF Royal Air Force — included airmen from Great Britain, New Zealand, Australia, Canada, South Africa, and from countries occupied by Germany (Netherlands, France, Belgium, Poland, Greece, and others).

Radio Oranje Escaping the Netherlands afterHitler's troops invaded, Queen Wilhelmina and other Dutch leaders waited out the war in London, England. Their radio broadcasts kept the Dutch people informed of the war's progress and boosted morale.

rationing Each registered Dutch citizen was only allowed a certain amount of bread, other foods, and clothing items each month.

resistors Men, women, and children secretly working against the Germans.

Sgt. Abbreviation for sergeant in the Army Air Corps.

SS - Schutzstaffel Hitler's elite Nazi unit in charge of concentration camps and rounding up Jews.

schule German for school.

scuttle Metal pail with a sloping side and lid — used to carry coal.

synagogue Jewish house of worship.

telefoon Dutch for telephone.

throttle Device controlling the flow of fuel or power to a plane's engine.

underground Men, women, and children secretly plotting against the Germans.

V-1 flying bomb Early form of cruise missile —Allied airmen based in England called them "buzz bombs" or "doodlebugs" when the bombs exploded near air bases.

war machine Armed forces of a country, along with industries and and networks that support them.

windmilling Spinning out of control.

SELECTED BIBLIOGRAPHY

FLIGHT

B-17 Flying Fortress "Nine-O-Nine." Wings of Freedom Tour, Collings
    Foundation. August, 2012.

INTERVIEWS

Berndien Geerlings (granddaughter of Dien and Herman Bosman).
    Dieren, Netherlands: November 12, 2013; September 6, 2015.
Mrs. Diet Geerlings-Bosman (daughter of Dien and Herman Bosman).
    Dieren, Netherlands: November 12, 2013; September 6, 2015.
Gerrit Jansen (son of *Villa Bergstein's* head gardener during WWII).
    Conducted by John Striker, Ellecom, Netherlands: August 21,
    2014.
Jack Kerpen (son of 2Lt. Robert Kerpen, bombardier on The Saint and
    Ten Sinners). Branford, CT: October 12, 2015.
Ralph Levie & Marcella Levie (son and daughter of Joop Levie).
    Amsterdam, Netherlands: April 25, 2014.
Arie van Veelen. Dieren, Netherlands: September 10, 2015.
Paul Versluys (guide, Museum Airfield Deelen), Arnhem, Netherlands:
    September 12, 2015.

DVD

Levie, Joop. *Interview 6151. Visual History Archive.* USC Shoah
Foundation. 2011. (translation by Berndien Geerlings).

ARTICLES

"Lt. Butterfoss Tells of Experience with 'Underground' in Holland."
    Hunterdon County Democrat. Flemington, NJ: July 5, 1945.
Pols, Menno. "*Na zestig jaar terug bij het 'jodenhol.'*" *de Gelderlander.*
    Gelderland, Netherlands: December 19, 2009. ("After Sixty
    Years, Back by the 'Jodenhol'").
Beuving, Tieme. "*Once winkel een verhaal rond een onderduikershol in de bossen
    van Middachten.*" *Ambt en Heerlijkheld.* Velp, Netherlands: March,
    2007. ("Our Shop: A Story around a Smuggler's Den in the

Forest of Middachten").

Reitsma, Jelle. "The Adventures of Lieutenant Donald E. Butterfoss and the Other Crew Members of 'The Saint and Ten Sinners.'" Apeldoorn, Netherlands: November 6, 2013.

Striker, John. "Piet Meijer: A Local Hero from the Resistance." Ellecom, Netherlands: October 22, 2015.

BOOKS

Boas, Jacob. *Boulevard des Misères: The Story of Transit Camp Westerbork*. Hamden, CO: Archon Books, 1985.

Bowman, Martin W. *The Mighty Eighth at War: US 8th Air Force Bombers versus the Luftwaffe 1943-1945*. South Yorkshire, England: Pen & Sword Books, Ltd., 2010.

Burton, Paul. *Escape from Terror*. Nederland, TX: Looking Glass Media, 1995.

Casey, Donald E. *To Fight for My Country, Sir! Memoirs of a 19 Year Old B-17 Navigator Shot Down in Nazi Germany and Imprisoned in the WWII "Great Escape" Prison Camp*. Chicago, IL: Sterling Cooper Publishing, 2009.

Closway, Gordon R. *Pictorial Record of the 401st Bomb Group*. San Angelo, TX: Newsfoto Publishing, Co., 1946.

Dorr, Robert F. *Mission to Berlin: The American Airmen Who Struck at the Heart of Hitler's Reich*. Minneapolis, MN: Zenith Press, 2011.

Frank, Anne. *Anne Frank: The Diary of a Young Girl*. New York, NY: Bantam Books, 1967. (translation by B. M. Mooyaart-Doubleday).

Freeman, Roger A. *The Mighty Eighth War Manual*. London, England: Cassel, 2001.

Goodman, W. E. 'Bill.' *Of Stirlings and Stalags: An Air-gunner's Tale*. London, England: PublishNation, 2013.

Greening, Col. C. Ross. *Not as Briefed: From the Doolittle Raid to a German Stalag*. Pullman, WA: Washington State University Press, 2001.

Grilley, Robert. *Return from Berlin: The Eye of a Navigator*. Madison, WI: The University of Wisconsin Press, 2003.

Hutchinson, James Lee. *The Boys in the B-17: 8th Air Force Combat Stories of WWII*. Bloomington, IN: AuthorHouse, 2011.

Ippisch, Hanneke. *SKY: A True Story of Courage during World War II*. New York, NY: Scholastic, Inc., 2007.

James, B. A. *Moonless Night: One Man's Struggle for Freedom 1940-1945*. Anstey, England: F. A. Thorpe (Publishing) Ltd. 1993.

Levine, Karen. *Hana's Suitcase: A True Story*. Morton Grove, IL: Albert Whitman & Company, 2002.

Meurs, John. *Not Home for Christmas: A Day in the Life of the Mighty Eighth*. Brandon, MS: Quail Ridge Press, 2009.

Miller, Donald L. *Masters of the Air: America's Bomber Boys Who Fought the Air War Against Nazi Germany*. New York, NY: Simon & Schuster Paperbacks, 2006.

Mulder, Dirk. *Camp Westerbork: Symbol of Destruction*. Hooghalen, Netherlands: Remembrance Center, 2003. (translation by Dr. L. Houwen & S. Bruidegom)

Neary, Bob. *Stalag Luft III: Sagan… Nuernberg… Moosburg*. North Wales, PA: 1946.

Parker, Ray. *Down In Flames: A True Story*. Minneapolis, MN: Mill City Press, Inc. 2009.

Perl, Lila and Marion Blumenthal Lazan. *Four Perfect Pebbles: A Holocaust Story*. New York, NY: Greenwillow Books, 1996.

Presser, Joseph, Dr. *Ashes in the Wind: The Destruction of Dutch Jewry*. London, England: Souvenir Press Ltd, 1965, 2010.

Schogt, Henry G. *The Curtain: Witness and Memory in Wartime Holland*. Waterloo, Canada: Wilfrid Laurier University Press, 2003.

Sweeting, C. G. *Combat Flying Equipment: U. S. Army Aviator's Personal Equipment 1917 - 1945*. Washington, D.C.: Smithsonian Institute, 1994.

van Tol, Ineke. *Persecution and Resistance in Amsterdam: A Walk from the Anne Frank House to the Dutch Resistance Museum*. Amsterdam, Netherlands: *Verzetmuseum*, 2006. (translation by Marieke Piggott).

van der Zee, Henri A. *The Hunger Winter: Occupied Holland 1944 -1945*. Lincoln, NE: University of Nebraska Press, 1982.

Walton, Marilyn Jeffers and Michael C. Eberhardt. *From Interrogation to Liberation: A Photographic Journey - Stalag Luft III - The Road to Freedom*. Bloomington, IN: AuthorHouse, 2014.

WEBSITES

"Anne Frank Timeline." www.annefrank.org/en/Subsites/Timeline/#.

"Anne's ID Card - Anne Frank Guide." www.annefrankguide.net/en-us/bronnenk.asp?aid=26318.

Backer-Gray, Barbara. "The Netherlands in World War II." residentalien.co/history.

"*Dulag Luft*." American Prisoners of War in Germany. Military

Intelligence Service, War Department 15 July 1944.
www.486th.org/Photos/Stammlager/KU3738/DulagLuft.htm.

"Ellecom 60 Years After." War Stories from Ellecom. www.zadelhof.nl.

Hatton, Greg (compiler). "American Prisoners of War in Germany:
Dulag Luft." WWW.B24.NET: Second Generation Research.
www.b24.net.

"The Hunger Winter." Dutch Resistance Museum. www.verzetmuseum.
org.

Lankford, Jim. "The Liberation of VII A." Moosburg Online.
www.moosburg.org.

"The Luftwaffe Interrogators at Dulag Luft — Oberursel." World War
II — Prisoners of War — Stalag Luft I. www.merkki.com.

"Mission #57 Reports." 401st Bombardment Group (Heavy)
Association. www.401stbg.org.

"Mission #60 Reports." 401st Bombardment Group (Heavy)
Association. www.401stbg.org.

"Netherlands Forced Labor - WWII." www.documentatiegroep40-45.
nlsdwangarbeid.

"Pilot Training Manual for the Flying Fortress. B-17. Revised 1 May,
1945 - for Headquarters, AAF." Aviationshoppe Historical
Archive. aviationshoppe.com/manuals/b17_wwii_manual/b17.
html.

Purner, David. "Down on 29 April 1944 - Mission: Berlin." WWW.B24.
NET: Second Generation Research. www.b24.net.

"Righteous Among the Nations: Bosman Family: Bosman Herman,
Bosman Dina, wife." www.yadvashem.org.

"Speeches for Radio Oranje." Koninklijke Bibiotheek (National Library of
the Netherlands). www.kb.nl.

"Squadron History - Part 2 March - April - May 1944." 613th
Bombardment Squadron (H). www.401bg.org.

"Stalag Luft 3." American Prisoners of War in Germany. Military
Intelligence Service, War Department. July 15, 1944. www.
486th.org.

Tison, Annette. "The Berlin Bombing Mission Flown by the Eighth Air
Force on April 29, 1944." www.b24.net/stories/annette.htm.

"To camp Westerbork." The Story of Anne Frank. www.annefrank.org.

Turchansky, Lorraine. "Sixty Years Ago, Canadians Liberated Nazi
Camp that Sent Thousands to their Deaths." Canadian Press,
April 7, 2005. www.militaryphotos.net.

"Westerbork Concentration Camp." www.fold3.com.

Woolf, Linda M. PhD. "Survival and Resistance: The Netherlands under Nazi Occupation." www2.webster.edu.

MUSEUM & OTHER VISITS

Airborne Museum
Airborne Museum
Oosterbeek, Netherlands

Joods Historisch Museum
Jewish Historical Museum
Amsterdam, Netherlands

Museum Vliegbasis Deelen
Museum Airfield Deelen
Arnhem, Netherlands

Paardestal (stable)
Hotel de Valkenberg
Rheden, Netherlands

Anne Frank Huis
Anne Frank House
Amsterdam, Netherlands

Kamp Westerbork
Camp Westerbork
Hooghalen, Netherlands

Nederlands Openluchmuseum
Netherlands Open Air Museum
Arnhem, Netherlands

Verzetsmuseum
Dutch Resistance Museum
Amsterdam, Netherlands

NOTES

Eighth Air Force Base 128, Deenethorpe, England, 29 April 1944, 0640 hours

1 Mission #60 Reports, <u>401st BG (H) Association</u>, 11. 21/9/15.

Ellecom, Netherlands, 29 April 1944, about 08:00 hours

2 "Netherlands Forced Labor - WWII." <u>www.documentatiegroep40-45.nlsdwangar</u>
<u>beid</u>. 16-9-15
More than 500,000 Dutch men, women, and teenagers were shipped to Germany to
work in war factories. More than 30,000 never returned home.

3 Queen Wilhelmina fled the Netherlands as Hitler's troops attacked on 10 May 1940.
She and the Dutch government sailed across the North Sea on the British destroyer,
HMS Hereward. She spent most of the war in London, England.

Ellecom, Netherlands, 29 April 1944, 12:30 hours

4 Tieme Beuving. *"Once winkel een verhaal rond een onderduikershol in de bossen van
Middachten." Ambt en Heerlijkheld.* (Velp, Netherlands: March, 2007), 2, 3.
Tieme Beuving dug the hole, along with friends Henk Wolf of Dieren and Piet Meijer,
who lived with his family at Hotel Brinkhorst in Ellecom. Tieme drew this sketch.

5 John Striker. "Piet Meijer: A Local Hero from the Resistance." (Ellecom,
Netherlands: October 22, 2015), 1, 2.
In January, 1944, Piet Meijer and his two friends were caught holding up an armory.
They were questioned about a hiding hole, then released. Picked up a few days later,
Piet was taken into the forest, where foresters who worked nearby were being held
hostage. Germans tortured him and threatened to shoot the men if Piet did not show
them the hole. After leading them there, he was sent to a German labor camp. In
March 1945, he escaped, but became trapped between American and German forces.
Taking cover in a barn, he was shot dead in a crossfire.

High over the Netherlands, 29 April 1944, 1450 hours

6 "Mission #57 Reports," <u>401st BG (H) Association</u>, www.401stbg.org, 10. 13/8/15.
Briefing officer for mission on 26 April 1944, emphasized three points for men who
went down on the mission. "Head for Holland and then into Belgium to France and
into Spain. Best method of travel is by bike - don't steal one. Most Dutch will help."

Ellecom, Netherlands, 30 April 1944, 04:00 hours

7 Interview with Diet Geerlings-Bosman. Dieren, Netherlands: November 12, 2013.

Ellecom, Netherlands, 30 April 1944, 12:30 hours

8 Interview with Diet Geerlings-Bosman. Ibid.

9 B. A. James. *Moonless Night: One Man's Struggle for Freedom 1940-1945.* (Anstey, England: F. A. Thorpe [Publishing], Ltd. 1993), 10.
This phrase appears here and in many accounts of downed Allied airmen.

Amsterdam, Netherlands, 1 May 1944, early evening

10 "*Dulag Luft.*" American Prisoners of War in Germany. Military Intelligence Service, War Department, July 15, 1944. www.486th.org/Photos/Stammlager/KU3738/Dulag Luft.htm. 3/4/15.

Dulag Luft, Transit Camp Air, Oberursel, Germany, mid-May 1944

11 "*Dulag Luft.*" Ibid., 2.

Ellecom, Netherlands, 18 November 1944, mid-afternoon

12 Bep's boyfriend, Jan Remmelink, lived in Dieren with his parents. His family ran a garage. In April, 1943, Jan drove the Levies to *Benvenuto* to go into hiding.

Ellecome, Netherlands, 25 December 1944, 13:00 hours

13 "The Hunger Winter." Dutch Resistance Museum. www.verzetmuseum.org. 9/5/15. Furious at the railroad strike supporting the Allied push into the Netherlands in fall of 1944, Germans cut supplies to western cities. More than 20,000 people died in *de hongerwinter.*

Dieren, Netherlands, 31 December 1944, afternoon

14 The sisters Witké, Truus and Grada, hid Rosa and Joop after the Green Police caught Salomon. Their house was across the street from the Levie's store, De Magneet.

De Steeg, Netherlands, 16 April 1945, 07:00 hours

15 Though Joop did not marry his daughter Willy (Wilhelmina) after the war, Mr. Berveling and Joop remained good friends.

Ellecom, Netherlands, 5 May 1945, mid-morning

16 "Speeches for *Radio Oranje.*" *Koninklijke Bibiotheek* (National Library of the Netherlands). www.kb.nl.

After the War

17 *Kamp Westerbork*, visit - 7/9/15.
Display states that 91,545 Jews left *Kamp Westerbork* aboard transit trains for *Auschwitz* and other concentration camps in eastern Europe. Little more than 5,000 returned.

IMAGE CREDITS

Courtesy Collection 401st Bomb Group (H) Assoc.: pages 9, 17, 29, 175, 179.

Courtesy Collection Jill Bateman, Landisville, PA: cover, pages 1, 10, 22, 24, 50, 79, 94, 139, 161 (2), 176 (2), 176 (2), 177, 178.

Courtesy Collection Berndien Geerlings, Dieren, Netherlands: cover, pages 5, 158.

Courtesy Gelders Archief, Arnhem, Netherlands: page 104 (1560-2134); page 153 (1540-7671).

Courtesy Historical Society Rheden-Rozendaal, Netherlands: page 40.

Image Bank WW2 - NIOD, Amsterdam, Netherlands: pages 74, 115, 141, 163.

Imperial War Museums, London, England: page 12 (© FRE 1272).

Courtesy Jewish Historical Museum, Amsterdam, Netherlands: pages 39, 156. (from photo album of Mrs. Betsy Pannekoek-Wessels, Dieren, Netherlands).

Courtesy Collection Kerpen Family, Branford, CT: pages 91, 98, 176 (2), 180.

Courtesy Collection Ralph Levie, Amsterdam, Netherlands: cover, pages 20, 65, 157(2).

Courtesy of the National WWII Museum, New Orleans, LA: page 93.

Courtesy Collection Stanley Family, Hampton, VA: page 176.

Courtesy Collection John Striker, Ellecom, Netherlands: page 73.

Courtesy Collection Arie and Marion van Veelen, Dieren, Netherlands: page 38.

Courtesy Washington State University Press, Pullman, WA: page 13. "The Fortress." Illustration by Colonel C. Ross Greening from the book, Not as Briefed: From the Doolittle Raid to a German Stalag. Pullman, WA: Washington State University Press, 2001.

Courtesy Collection William Watkins Family, Huntington Beach, CA: page 176.

Courtesy USAFA McDermott Library MS 329, CO: cover, pages 87, 97, 145, 147, 149, 151.

Public Domain: cover (B-17), pages 15, 28, 33, 84, 102, 180* (all from Wikipedia). *Anne Frank photograph is in United States public domain because in Dutch and American copyright laws, a photograph taken by an unknown photographer before 1943 exceeds the 70 years protected by copyright laws.

© Linda Berry, Lancaster, PA: cover, pages, 7, 18-19, 26-27, 46-47, 121, 125.

BUTTERFOSS CREW

Crew of The Saint and Ten Sinners

Back row - left to right:
  Staff Sgt. Alfred J. Truskowski - Flight Engineer - POW in *Stalag Luft IV*.
  Sgt. Everett W. Stanley - Ball Turret Gunner - POW in *Stalag Luft IV*.
  Staff Sgt. Roger R. McCauley - Radio Operator - POW in *Stalag Luft IV*.
  Sgt. John W. Reeves - Right Waist Gunner - POW in *Stalag Luft IV*.
  Sgt. William E. Watkins - Left Waist Gunner - Evaded capture.
  Sgt. William H. Lee - Tail Gunner - POW in *Stalag Luft IV*.

Front row - left to right:
  2Lt. Donald E. Butterfoss - Pilot - POW in *Stalag Luft III*.
  2Lt. Robert L. Westfall - Copilot - POW in *Stalag Luft III*.
  Flight Officer Bernard J. Boyle (not pictured). Pictured is 2Lt. Roy H. Lang of
    Cincinnati, Ohio, the crew's original navigator who fell ill and could not travel
    to England. Boyle replaced him as navigator - POW in *Stalag Luft III*.
  2Lt. Robert C. Kerpen - Bombardier - POW in *Stalag Luft III*.

The Butterfoss crew dumped their duffle bags in a quonset hut at Deenethorpe,
England, on 26 March 1944 — Butter's twenty-second birthday. On 26 April, they
bombed factories in Brunswick, Germany, while flying Fitch's Bandwagon. On 29
April, Butter's crew flew their second mission and last mission. Returning crews
reported flak was extremely heavy over Berlin that day. The Saint was one of sixty-
three bombers lost by the Eighth Air Force on this mission.

CREW MEMORABILIA

1 — German identification document for Flight Officer Bernard Boyle.
2 — Sgt. Everett Stanley returning stateside, most likely at Baltimore, Maryland.
3 — Lt. Butterfoss, Lt. Kerpen, and Lt. Westfall before shipping overseas.
4 — Lt. Robert Kerpen's ID card from *Stalag Luft III*.
5 —19-year-old Sgt. "Bill" Watkins sends love to his 17-year-old bride back home.
6 — Telegram notifying Butter's family he was a prisoner of war.

BEP BOSMAN'S LETTER, 1948

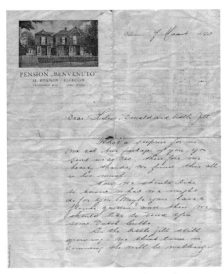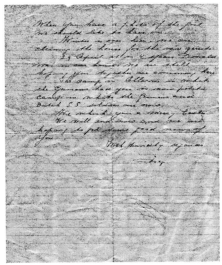

Only surviving letter from the Bosmans to Butter and his family in the USA.
The letter serves as background for the book jacket,
and its letterhead helped the author find the Bosman family.

7 March 1948

Dear Helene, Donald and little Jill,

What a surprise for us. We got two packages of you, you sent us 20 Dec. Therefore
  our hearty thanks. We find this all too much.
Now we should like to know what we might do for you. Maybe you have a flower
  garden? And then we should like to send you some Dutch bulbs.
Is the little Jill still growing up? We think time is coming she will be walking.
When you have a photo of the girl we should like to have one.
Winter is over here, we are cleaning the house for the new guests.
29 April it is 4 years Donald was in our house. We are still hoping you together are
  coming here.
The camp in Ellecom in which the Germans had you is now a politic camp in which
  the Germans and Dutch *SS* soldiers are now.
We wish you a merry Easter.
We will end now and we are hoping to get some good news of you.

With kindly regards,
Bep

ACKNOWLEDGMENTS

It was time. Two and a half years ago, it was time to find the "nice Dutch family who played hide-and-seek" with my father in WWII. My clues consisted of two names — H. Bosman and Ellecom — taken from the letterhead of a wrinkled letter sent from the Netherlands in 1948.

Neither name stirred up interest on the Internet. However, typing in Butterfoss and B-17 led to retired Brigadier General Jelle Reitsma, who led to John Striker, Ellecom's Town Historian, who led to Diet Geerlings-Bosman and her daughter, Berndien, who led to Ralph Levie and his sister Marcella.

The rest is history, as people say.
Literally, H I S T O R Y.

We have been wrapped in World War II ever since. As it turns out, Jelle, John, Diet, Berndien, Ralph, Marcella, and my husband — whose father is still MIA from WWII — make a remarkable research team.

Others have joined us on the journey. Don Byers and Ralph Bellamy added knowledge and photographs of Butter's 401st Bomb Group. Dr. Mary Elizabeth Ruwell, Academy Archivist at the USAF Academy's McDermott Library, provided numerous photographs of *Stalag Luft III*. The Stanley, Watkins, and Kerpen families chipped in details and memorabilia to add to the story of the B-17 and its crew. Devorah Winegarten of Texas cheerfully served as a terrific mentor for the task of publishing one's own book.

Family members have contributed as well. Son Jeff offered loyal support. Daughter Julie and husband Jeff lent their professional expertise. Grandsons Drew and Ryan eagerly shared their kids' perspective.

One of the most gratifying experiences was meeting Dien and Herman's grown grandchildren at their family reunion in Dieren, Netherlands. Speaking on behalf of the Bosman family, Berndien Geerlings declared, "We are so proud and grateful that this true war story has been told and preserved for all future generations to understand."

Berndien Geerlings is second from the
right in the back row.

FLYING FORTS
IN THE CLASSROOM

WHAT WOULD YOU HAVE DONE?

If you and your family lived in the Netherlands during WWII,
  what choices would you have made?
Would you have joined the underground?
Would you have hidden a Jewish family in your attic?
Would you have done nothing to help those around you?
Would you have collaborated with the enemy?

WHO WERE THE HEROES?

Discuss what is a hero?
What are the characteristics one needs to be a hero?
Who is the hero in the story?
Is there more than one hero in the story? If so, who are they?
Does doing one's job make one a hero?
Can someone wear the enemy's uniform and still act like a hero?

DID YOU NOTICE?

On the map of the Bail-Out Zone (pages 46-47), can you figure out which parachute was Butter's? Can you find Butter running through the trees?

On the map of Ellecom (pages 26-27), can you find Butter running through the trees? Did you trace the three different routes Butter took in his short time in Ellecom?

Can you find words referring to characters and setting on the cover?

Who is looking out *Benvenuto's* round window on page 7?

Read Bep's letter on page 177 to find out what happened to Dutch blackcoats.

One word serves as a metaphor for war throughout the story. It is found in every chapter except the first. What it is? Why isn't it in the first chapter?

This is the emblem of Butter's 613th Bomb Squad of the 401st Bomb Group based in Deenethorpe, England. If you know who first drew Mickey Mouse, then you know who drew this boxing bomb. Walt Disney and his staff drew more than 1200 designs for US military units in WWII.

Lesson plan: Julie Mackneer, 5th grade teacher, Palmyra Area School District, PA.

MORE COMPELLING STORIES

From *Stalag Luft III*:

Tom, Dick, and Harry. Not prisoners, but escape tunnels dug by *kriegies* in North Compound — all three at the same time. German guards discovered Tom under barracks 123. Necessity turned Dick into a storage area. Yet, on the snowy night of 24 March 1944, bodies began squirming from a hole in the ground — the exit of the tunnel named Harry.

Read more about the Great Escape in

Front gate of Stalag Luft III. Sketched by Lt. Robert Kerpen on 17 August 1944.

The Tunnel King: The True Story of Wally Flood and the Great Escape, by Barbara Hehner, 2004.

The Great Escape: Tunnel to Freedom, by Mike Meserole, 2008.

From *Kamp Westerbork*:

A teenage girl, with hair black as coal, sat in the sunshine on a late August day in 1944. She did not fret about the camp's barbed wire fences, nor about living in the punishment block because her family had been *onderduikers*. Instead, she enjoyed being out in the fresh air and talking to other prisoners.

Read more about Anne Frank in

Anne Frank in 1940 at school in Amsterdam, Netherlands.

Anne Frank: The Diary of a Young Girl, by Anne Frank, 1993.

Anne Frank: The Anne Frank House Authorized Graphic Biography, by Sid Jacobson and Ernie Colón, 2010.

"Anne Frank Timeline" www.annefrank.org/en/Subsites/Timeline/#.

Anne Frank's ID www.annefrankguide.net/en-us/bronnenk.asp?aid=26318.